Methods of Teaching Computer

Methods of Teaching Computer

Deepak Tiwari

CRESCENT
PUBLISHING CORPORATION

[*The responsibility for the facts stated, conclusions reached and plagiarism, if any, in this book is entirely that of the Author. And the Publisher bears no responsibility for them, whatsoever.*]

Methods of Teaching Computer

First Published : **2014**

ISBN 81-8342-021-4

Published by :

CRESCENT PUBLISHING CORPORATION
4831/24, Prahlad Street,
Ansari Road, Darya Ganj,
New Delhi - 110002
Ph. : 23272541, 23257835
Fax : 91- 011- 23257835
e-mail : campusbooks@hotmail.com

Typesetting by :

Arjun Computers
Delhi - 110051

Printed at :
Roshan Offset Printers
Delhi

Preface

The introduction of computers into the classroom has been exciting, but many educators would probably agree that they have not seen the results we anticipated. Teachers, parents and school boards are beginning to question their investments in computer technology. Most students today are still educated the same way students were educated a generation or two ago. Recent studies reveals that computers were rarely used by school students, and when they were used, the primary type of software was drill and practice and educational games.

Individuals in the workplace are using computers as a tool while educators generally tend to think of computers as an instructional delivery device. This observation is interesting because if we asked why computers are being placed in the schools, the primary reason is to prepare students for the workforce—where computers are used as a tool.

This book is written for the pre-service and practising teacher who has very basic computer skills such as using a mouse; opening, creating, and saving documents; and using menus. It presents rich knowledge both about computer and about strategies and approaches to teach computer. It also shows how computers can enhance student motivation and engagement. Teachers will also learn from the book about the variety of computer software available for teaching reading at various levels.

Deepak Tiwari

Contents

	Preface	*v*
1.	Teaching Computer for Beginners	1
2.	Computer Use of Teachers	51
3.	Teaching Computer Programmes	76
4.	Online Teaching	134
5.	Assessing Computer Conferencing	172
6.	Enhancing Students' Creativity and Thinking Skills	195
7.	Interactive Education Technologies	217
8.	Online Course Design and Delivery	234
9.	Teacher Professional Engagement	245
	Bibliography	273
	Index	275

1

Teaching Computer for Beginners

There is clear and widespread agreement among the public and educators that all students need to be proficient computer users or "computer literate." However, while states are spending a great deal of money on technology, there seems to be only a vague notion of what computer literacy really means. Can the student who operates a computer well enough to play a game, send e-mail or surf the Web be considered computer literate? Will a student who uses computers in school only for running tutorials or an integrated learning system have the skills necessary to survive in our society? Will the ability to do basic word processing be sufficient for students entering the workplace or post-secondary education? Clearly not. In too many schools, teachers and students still use computers only as the equivalent of expensive flash cards, electronic worksheets, or as little more than a typewriter. The productivity side of computer use in the general content area curriculum is neglected or grossly underdeveloped.

Recent publications by educational associations are advocating for a more meaningful use of technology in schools. Educational technologists are clearly describing what students should know and be able to do with technology. They are advocating integrating computer skills into the content areas, proclaiming that computer skills should not be taught in isolation and that separate "computer classes" do not really help students learn to apply computer skills in meaningful ways. There is increasing recognition that the end result of computer literacy is not knowing how to operate computers, but to use technology as a tool for organization, communication, research, and problem solving. This is an important shift in approach and emphasis.

Moving from teaching isolated technology skills to an integrated approach is an important step that takes a great deal of planning and effort. Fortunately, we have a model for doing so. Over the past 25 years, library media professionals have worked hard to move from teaching isolated "library skills" to teaching integrated "information skills." They found that information skills can be integrated effectively when the skills (1) directly relate to the content area curriculum and to classroom assignments, and (2) are tied together in a logical and systematic information process model.

Schools seeking to move from isolated information technology skills instruction will also need to focus on both of these requirements. Successful integrated information skills programs are designed around collaborative projects jointly planned and taught by teachers and library media professionals. Information technology skills instruction can and should be imbedded in such a curriculum. Library media specialists, computer teachers, and classroom teachers need to work together to develop units and lessons that will include both technology skills, information skills, and content-area curriculum outcomes.

A meaningful, unified information technology literacy curriculum must be more than a "laundry list" of isolated skills, such as knowing the parts of the computer, writing drafts and final products with a word processor, and searching for information using the World Wide Web.

While these specific skills are important for students to learn, the "laundry list" approach does not provide an adequate model for students to transfer and apply skills from situation to situation. These curricula address the "how" of computer use, but rarely the "when" or "why." Students may learn isolated skills and tools, but they would still lack an understanding of how those various skills fit together to solve problems and complete tasks. Students need to be able to use computers and other technologies flexibly, creatively and purposefully.

All learners should be able to recognize what they need to accomplish, determine whether a computer will help them to do so, and then be able to use the computer as part of the process of accomplishing their task. Individual computer skills take on a new meaning when they are integrated within this type of information problem-solving process, and students develop true "information technology literacy" because they have genuinely applied various information technology skills as part of the learning process.

Some technology literacy competencies that may be relevant in some situations include:

(1) knowing the basic operation, terminology, and maintenance of equipment,

(2) knowing how to use computer-assisted instructional programs,

(3) having knowledge of the impact of technology on careers, society, and culture (as a direct instructional objective), and

(4) computer programming.

Defining and describing technology skills is only a first step in assuring all our children become proficient information and technology users. A teacher-supported scope and sequence of skills, well designed projects, and effective assessments are also critical. Equally essential is collaboration among classroom teachers, teacher librarians, and technology teachers in order to present students with a unified and integrated approach to ensure that all children master the skills they will need to thrive in an information rich future.

Data Collection

When programs are at most a couple of hundred lines, it doesn't much matter whether the data structures and associated functions are well defined. Such programs are so small that they are easy to "hack out" using any ad hoc approach that comes to mind. As you get on to larger programs, it becomes more and more essential to provide well defined groupings of data and associated functionality. This is particularly important if several people must collaborate to build a program. It isn't practical to have several people trying to develop the same piece of code, the code has to be split up so that each programmer gets specific parts to implement.

You may be able to split a program into separately implementable parts by considering the top level of a top-down functional decomposition. But usually, such parts are far from independent. They will need to share many different data structures Often lower levels of the decomposition process identify requirements for similar routines for processing these structures; this can lead to duplication of code or to inconsistencies. In practice, the individuals implementing different "top level functions" wouldn't be able to go off and proceed independently An alternative decomposition that focussed on the data might work better.

Consider the information retrieval example, you could give someone the task of building a "bit map component". This person would agree to provide a component that transferred bit maps between memory and disk, checked equality of bit maps, counted common bits in two maps, and performed any other necessary functions related to bit maps. Another component could have been a "text record component". This could have been responsible for displaying its contents, working with files, and (by curtesy of the bit map component) building a bit map that encoded the key words that were present in that text record.

The individuals developing these two components could work substantially independently. Some parts of a component might not be testable until all other components are complete and brought together but, provided that the implementors start by agreeing to the component interfaces, it is possible to proceed with the detailed design and coding of each component in isolation. A header file basically describes the form of a data structure and informs other programmers of some useful functions, already implemented, that can be used to manipulate such structures There is nothing to enforce controls; nothing to make programmers use the suggested interface. Of course, if implementors are to work on separate parts of a program, they must stick to the agreed interfaces.

Consider the example of programmers, A, B, C, and D who were working on a geometry modelling system. Programmer A was responsible for the coordinate component; this involved points (`struct pt { double x, y; };`) and functions like `offset_pt(double dx, double dy)`. Programmer B was uncooperative and did not want to wait for A to complete the points component Instead of using calls to offset `_pt()` `B` wrote code that manipulated the data fields directly (`pt p; ... p.x += d1;`). B then left the project and was replaced by D.

Programmer C needed polar coordinates and negotiated with A for functions radius `(const pt p)` and theta(const pt p). After implementing these functions, A and C did a timing analysis of their code and found that these new functions were being called very often and represented a measurable percentage of the run time Programmer A, who after all was officially responsible for the definition of points and their behaviour, updated things so that the struct contained polar as well as cartesian coordinates (`struct pt { double x, y, r, theta; };`).

A changed the new `radius()` and `theta()` functions so that these simply returned the values of the extra data members and then changed all the functions like `offset_pt()` so that these updated the polar coordinates as well as the cartesian coordinates Programmers C and D duly recompiled their parts to reflect the fact that the definition of struct pt had changed with the addition of the extra data members Programmer A was fired because the code didn't work. C and D wasted more than a week on A's code before they found the incorrect, direct usage of the struct in the code originally written by B.

The problem here was that A couldn't define a "wall" around the data of a point structure. The header file had to describe the structure as well as the prototypes of A's routines. Since the structure was known, uncooperative programmers like B could access it. Things would have been different if A could have specified things so that point structures could only be used via A's own routines. (In particular, A would still have a job, while B would probably have quit before the project really started.) Modern programs typically require many "components". These components consist of the declaration of new type of data object and of the functions that are to be used to manipulate instances of this new type. You do require "walls around the data". When you define a new data type, you should be able to specify how it is to be used. If you can define components like this, then you can expect to be able to put a program together by combining separately developed components that work in accord with specified interfaces.

It is possible use the older C language to implement components. Possible. But it is not always easy and it does depend on the discipline of the programmers. C doesn't enforce compliance with an interface. (One could argue that C doesn't enforce anything!) In contrast, the C++ language has extensive support for the programmer who needs to define and work with new data types. The new language feature of C++ that supports a component oriented style of programming is "class". A "class" is meant to describe a conceptual entity; that is describe something that owns data and provides services related to its data A class declaration defines a new data type. The declaration does specify the form of a data structure and in this respect it is like a struct declaration. Once the compiler has seen the class declaration, it permits the definition of variables of this new type; these variables are normally referred to as "instances of a class" or "objects".

In addition to describing the data members, a class declaration allows a programmer to specify how objects that are instances of the class can be used. This is done by identifying those functions that are allowed to access and change data members in an object. These functions are mainly "member functions". Member functions form part of the definition of the new data type. The code for member functions is not normally included in the class declaration Usually, a class declaration is in a header file; the code implementing the member functions will be in a separate code file (or files).

However, at the point where they are defined, member functions clearly identify the class of which they are a part Consequently, although the description of a class may be spread over a header file and several code files, it is actually quite easy to gather it all together in response to a request like "Show me how this code represents a 'Customer'."

Classes and Design

The major benefit of classes is that they encourage and support a "component oriented" view of program development. Program development is all about repeatedly reanalyzing a problem, breaking it down into smaller more manageable pieces that can be thought about independently. The decomposition process is repeated until you know you have identified parts that are simple enough to be coded, or which may already exist.

Components (and the classes that describe them) give you an additional way of breaking up a problem In fact, for large programs you should start by trying to identify the "components" needed in a program. You try to partition the problem into components that each own some parts of the overall data and perform all the operations needed on the data that they own. So you get "bit map" components, "hash table" components, "word" components and "text record" components. You characterize how the program works in terms of interactions among these components - e.g. "if the `hash_table` identifies a `vocab_item` that matches the word, then get the bit number from that `vocab_item` and ask the `bit_map` to set that bit".

You have to identify all uses of a component. This allows you to determine what data that component owns and what functions it performs Given this information, you can define the C++ class that corresponds to the identified component. Once you have completed an initial decomposition of the programming problem by identifying the required classes, you have to complete a detailed design for each one But each class is essentially a separate problem. Instead of one big complex programming problem, you now have lots little isolated subproblems. Once the data and member functions of a class have been identified, most of the work on the design of a class relates to the design and implementation of its individual member functions.

When you have reached the level of designing an individual member function of a class you are actually back in the same sort of situation. You have a tiny program to write. If a member function has a more complex task to perform, you may have to identify additional auxiliary functions that do part of its work. So, the techniques of top down functional decomposition come into play.

You consider coding the member function. You break the member function down into extra functions (each of which becomes an extra member function of the class) until you have simplified things to the point where you can implement directly using basic programming constructs Breaking a problem into separately analyzable component parts gives you a way of handling harder problems. But there are additional benefits. Once you start looking for component parts, you tend to find that your new program requires components that are similar to or identical to components that you built for other programs.

This is a bit like reusing algorithms by getting functions from a function library. However, the scale of reuse is greater. If you get a `sort()` function from a function library, you are reusing one function. If you get a ready built bitmap class, you get an integrated set of functions along with a model for a basic data structure that you require in your program. Increasingly, software developers are relying on "class libraries" that contain classes that define ready made versions of many commonly required components.

Class Declarations and Definition

A class declaration introduces the name of a new data type, identifies the data members present in each variable of this type (i.e. each "class instance" or "object"), identifies the member functions that may be used to manipulate such variables, and describes the access (security) controls that apply. A declaration has the form:

```
class Name {
details ...
more details ...
};
```

The declaration starts with the keyword `class`. The name of the class is then given The usual naming rules apply, the name starts with a letter and contains letters, digits and underscore characters. (Sometimes, there may be additional naming conventions Thus you may encounter an environment where you are expected to start the name of a class with either 'T' or 'C'.) The body of the declaration, with all the details, comes between `{` and `}` brackets The declaration ends with a semicolon.

Compilers get really upset, and respond with incomprehensible error messages, if you omit that final semicolon The details have to include a list of the associated functions and data members Initially the examples will be restricted slightly, the associated functions will all be "member functions", that is they all are functions that are inherently part of the definition of the concept represented by the class. These lists of member functions and data members also specify the access controls There are only two kinds of access that need be considered at this stage. They are defined by the keywords `public` and `private`.

A `public` member function (or data member) is one that can be used anywhere in the code of the program. A `private` data member (or member function) is one that can only be used within the code of the functions identified in the class declaration itself. Note the wording of the explanation Generally, data members are all `private`, there may also be a few `private` member functions. The main member functions are all `public` (sometimes, but very rarely, there may be `public` data members). You can specify the appropriate access control for each data member and member function individually, or you can have groups of `public` members interspersed with groups of `private` members. But most often, the following style is used:

```
class Name {
public:
details of the "public interface" of the
class
private:
private implementation details
and description of data members of each
instance
of the class...
};
```

In older text books, you may find the order reversed with the `private` section defined first. It is better to have the `public` interface first. Someone who wants to know how Keywords 'public' and 'private' to use objects of this class need only read the public interface and can stop reading at the keyword .

The following examples are just to make things a little more concrete. First, there is a class defining the concept of a point in two dimensional space (such as programmer A, from the earlier example, might have wished to define):

```
class Point {
public:
...
// Get cartesian coords
double X();
double Y();
// Get polar coords
```

```
double Radius();
double Theta();
// Test functions
int ZeroPoint();
int InFirstQuad();
...
// Modify
void Offset(double deltaX, double deltaY);
...
void SetX(double newXval);
...
// Comparisons
int Equal(const Point& other);
...
private: void FixUpPolarCoords();
...
double fX, fY, fR, fTheta;
};
```

(The ellipses, "...", indicate places where additional member functions would appear in actual class declaration; e.g. there would be several other test functions, hence the ellipsis after function `InFirstQuad()`. The ellipsis after the public keyword marks the place where some special initialization functions would normally appear. The `public` interface specifies what other programmers can do with variables that are instances of this type (class). Points can be asked where they are, either in cartesian or polar coordinate form. Points can be asked whether they are at the coordinate origin or whether they are in a specified quadrant (functions like `ZeroPoint()` and `InFirstQuad()`). Points can be asked to modify their data members using functions like `Offset()`. They may also be asked to compare themselves with other points through functions like `Equal()`.

The private section of the class declaration specifies things that are concern of the programmer who implemented the class and of no one else. The data members generally appear here. In this case there are the duplicated coordinate details - both cartesian and polar versions. For the class to work correctly, these data values must be kept consistent at all times.

There could be several functions that change the cartesian coordinate values (`Offset()`, `SetX()` etc). Every time such a change is made, the polar coordinates must also be updated. During the detailed design of the class, the code that adjusts the polar coordinates would be abstracted out of the functions like `SetX()`. The code becomes the body for the distinct member function `FixUpPolarCoords()` This function is private. It is an implementation detail. It should only be called from within those member functions of the class that change the values of the cartesian coordinates. Other programmers using points should never call this function; as far as they are concerned, a point is something that always has consistent values for its polar and cartesian coordinates.

For a second example, how about class `Customer:`

```
class Customer {
public:

   ...
```

```
    // Disk transfers
    int ReadFrom(ifstream& input);
    int WriteTo(ofstream& output);
    // Display
    void PrintDetails(ofstream& out);
    // Query functions
    int Debtor();
    ...
    // Changes
    void GetCustomerDetails();
    void GetOrder();
    ...
  private:
    UT_Word         fName;
    ...
    UT_Word         fOrders[kMAXITEMS];
    int             fNumOrder;
    double          fAmountOwing;
    Date            fLastOrder;
  };
```

The data members in this example include arrays and a struct as well as simple data types like int and double. This is normal; class `Point` is atypical in having all its data members being variables of built in types. There is no requirement that the data members have names starting with 'f'. It is simply a useful convention that makes code easier to read and understand. A name starting with 'g' signifies a global variable, a name with 's' is a "file scope" static variable, 'e' implies an enumerator, 'c' or 'k' is a constant, and 'f' is a data member of a class or struct. There are conventions for naming functions but these are less frequently adhered to.

Functions that ask for yes/no responses from an object (e.g. `Debtor()` or In `FirstQuad()`) are sometimes given names that end with '_p' (e.g `Debtor_p()`); the 'p' stands for "predicate" (dictionary: 'predicate' assert or affirm as true or existent). `ReadFrom()` and `WriteTo()` are commonly used as the names of the functions that transfer objects between memory and disk. Procedures (void functions) that perform actions may all have names that involve or start with "Do" (e.g. `DoPrintDetails()`). You will eventually convince yourself of the value of such naming conventions; just try maintaining some code where no conventions applied.

Defining the Member Functions

A class declaration promises that the named functions will be defined somewhere Actually, you don't have to define all the functions, you only have to define those that get used. This allows you to develop and test a class incrementally. You will have specified the class interface, with all its member functions listed, before you start coding; but you can begin testing the code as soon as you have a reasonable subset of the functions defined.

Usually, class declarations go in header files, functions in code files. If the class represents a single major component of the program, e.g. `class Customer`, you will probably have a header file Customer.h and an implementation file Customer.cp Something less important, like class `Point`, would probably be declared in a header file ("geom.h") along with several related classes (e.g. `Point3D, Rectangle, Arc, ...`) and the definitions of the member functions of all these classes would be in a corresponding geom.cp file. A member function definition has the general form:

```
return type
class_name::function_name(arguments)
{
body of function
}
```

e.g.

```
void Customer::PrintDetails(ofstream& out)
{
...
}
double
Point::Radius()
{
...
}
```

(Some programmers like the layout style where the return type is on a separate line so that the class name comes at the beginning of the line.) The double colon :: is the "scope qualifier" operator. Although there are other uses, the main use of this operator is to associate a class name with a function name when a member function is being defined. The definitions of all functions of class Point will appear in the form `Point::function_name`, making them easy to identify even if they occur in a file along with other definitions like `Point3D::Radius()` or `Arc::Arc-Angle()`).

Some examples of function definitions are:

```
double Point::Radius()

{

return fR;

}

void Point::SetX(double newXval)

{

fX = newXval;

FixUpPolarCoords();

}

void Point::Offset(double deltaX, double
deltaY)

{

fX += deltaX;

fY += deltaY;

FixUpPolarCoords();

}
```

Now you may find something slightly odd about these definitions. The code is simple enough. `Offset()` just changes the `fX` and `fY` fields of the point and then calls the private member function `FixUpPolar Coords()` to make the fR, and fTheta members consistent. The oddity is that it isn't clear which Point object is being manipulated. After all, a program will have hundreds of Points as individual variables or elements of arrays of Points. Each one of these points has its own individual fX and fY data members.

The code even looks as if it ought to be incorrect, something that a compiler should stomp on. The names fX and fY are names of data members of something that is like a struct, yet they are being used on their own while in all previous examples we have only used member names as parts of fully qualified names (e.g. thePt.fX) If you had been using the constructs illustrated and you could have had a struct Pt and function OffsetPt() and FixPolars():

```
struct Pt { double x, y, r, t; }; void
OffsetPt(Pt& thePoint, double dx, double dy)
{
thePoint.x += dx;
thePoint.y += dy;
FixPolars(thePoint);
}
void FixPolars(Pt& thePt)
{
...
}
```

The functions that change the Pt struct have a Pt& (reference to Pt) argument; the value of this argument determines which Pt struct gets changed This is obviously essential. These functions change structs (or class instances). The functions have to have an argument identifying the one that is to be changed. However, no such argument is apparent in the class member function definitions The class member functions do have an implicit extra argument that identifies the object being manipulated. The compiler adds the address of the object to the list of arguments defined in the function prototype.

The compiler also modifies all references to data members so that they become fully qualified names Rather than a reference parameter like that in the functions `OffsetPt()` and `FixPolars()` just shown, this extra parameter is a "pointer". They are basically just addresses (as are reference parameters) However, the syntax of code using pointers is slightly different. In particular a new operator, ->, is introduced. This "pointer operator" is used when accessing a data member of a structure identified by a pointer variable. A few examples appear in the following code. You can imagine the compiler as systematically changing the function prototypes and definitions. So, for example:

```
void Point::SetX(double newXval)
{
fX = newXval;
FixUpPolarCoords();
}
```

gets converted to

```
void __Point__SetX_ptsd(Point* this, double
newXval)
{
```

```
this->fX = newXval;
this->FixUpPolarCoords();
}
```

while

```
int Customer::Debtor()
{
return (fAmountOwing > 0.0);
}
```

gets converted to

```
int __Customer__Debtor_ptsv(Customer* this)
{
return (this->fAmountOwing > 0.0);
}
```

The `this` pointer argument will contain the address of the data, so the compiler can generate code that modifies the appropriate `Point` or checks the appropriate `Customer` Normally, you leave it to the compiler to put in "`this->`" in front of every reference to a data member or member function; but you can write the code with the "`this->`" already present. Sometimes, the code is easier to understand if the pointer is explicitly present.

Using Class Instances

Once a class declaration has been read by the compiler (usually as the result of processing a #include directive for a header file with the declaration), variables of that class type can be defined:

```
#include "Customer.h"
...
void RunTheShop()
{
Customer theCustomer;
...
}
```

or

```
#include "geom.h"
void DrawLine(Point& p1, Point& p2)
{
Point MidPoint;
...
}
```

Just like structs, variables of class types can be defined, get passed to functions by value or by reference, get returned as a result of a function, and be copied in assignment statements. Most code that deals with structs consists of statements that access and manipulate individual data members, using qualified names built up with the "." operator. Thus in previous examples we have had things like:

```
cout << theVocabItem.fWord;
strcpy(theTable[ndx].fWord, aWord);
```

With variables of class types you can't go around happily accessing and changing their data; the data are walled off! You have to ask a class instance to change its data or tell you about the current data values:

```
Point thePoint;
...
thePoint.SetX(5.0);
...
if(thePoint.X() < 0.0) ...
```

These requests, calls to member functions, use much the same syntax as the code that accessed data members of structures. A call uses the name of the object qualified by the name of the function (and its argument list). You can guess how the compiler deals with things. You already know that the compiler has built a function:

```
void __Point__SetX_ptsd(Point* this, double
newXval);
```

from the original void Point::SetX(double). A call like

```
thePoint.SetX(5.0);
```

gets converted into:

```
__Point__SetX_ptsd(&thePoint, 5.0);
```

(The & "get the address of" operator is again used here to obtain the address of the point that is to be changed. This address is then passed as the value of the implicit `Point* this` parameter.)

Initialization and "constructor" functions

Variables should be initialized. Previous examples have shown initialization of simple variables, arrays of simple variables, structs, and arrays of structs. Class instances also need to be initialized. For classes like class `Point` and class `Customer`, initialization would mean setting values in data fields. Instances of "resource manager" classes can be responsible for much more than a small collection of data; there are classes whose instances own opened files, or that control Internet connections to programs running on other computers, or which manage large collections of other data objects either in memory or on disk. Initialization for instances of these more complex structures may involve performing actions in addition to setting a few values in data members.

So as to accommodate these more complex requirements, C++ classes define special initialization functions. These special functions are called "constructors" because they are invoked as an instance of the class is created (or constructed) There are some special rules for contructors. The name of the function is the same as the name of the class. A constructor function does not have any return type.

We could have:

```
class Point {

public:

Point(double initalX = 0.0, double initialY
= 0.0);

...

};

class Customer {

public:

Customer();

...

};
```

The constructor for class Point has two arguments, these are the initial values for the X, Y coordinates. Default values have been specified for these in the declaration The constructor for class Customer takes no arguments. These functions have to have definitions:

```
Point::Point(double initialX, double
initialY)
{
fX = initialX;
fY = initialY;
FixUpPolarCoords();
}
constructors
Customer::Customer()
{
strcpy(fName, "New customer");
strcpy(fAddress, "Delivery address");
...
fAmountOwing = 0.0;
}
```

Here, the constructors do involve calls to functions. The constructor for class `Point` initializes the `fX, fY` data members but must also make the polar coordinates consistent; that can be accomplished by a call to the member function `FixUpPolar-Coords()`. The constructor for `Customer` makes calls to `strcpy` from the string library A class can have an overloaded constructor; that is there can be more than one constructor function, with the different versions having different argument lists. Constructors can get quite elaborate and can acquire many specialized forms

When you need to define intialized instances of a class, you specify the arguments for the constructor function in the definition of the variable. For example:

```
Point p1(17.0, 0.5);

Point p2(6.4);

Point p3;
```

Variable `p1` is a Point initially located at 17.0, 0.5; `p2` is located at 6.4, 0.0 (using the default 0.0 value for `initialY`). `Point p3` is located at 0.0, 0.0 (using the defaults for both `initialX` and `initialY`).

Const Member Functions

Some member functions change objects, others don't. For example:

```
double Point::Y()

{

return fY;

}
```

doesn't change the `Point` for which this function is invoked; whereas the `Point` is changed by

```
: void Point::SetY(double newYval)

{

fY = newYval;

FixUpPolarCoords();

}
```

It is worthwhile making this clear in the class declaration:

```
class Point {
public:
    ...
    // Get cartesian coords
    double X() const;
    double Y() const;
    // Get polar coords
    double Radius() const;
    double Theta() const;
    // Test functions
    int ZeroPoint() const;
    int InFirstQuad() const;
    ...
    // Modify
    void Offset(double deltaX, double
    deltaY);
    void SetX(double newXval);
    ...
    // Comparisons
    int Equal(const Point& other) const;
```

Functions that don't change the object should be qualified by the keyword const both in the declaration, and again in their definitions:

```
double Point::Radius() const
```

```
{
return fR;
}
```

Apart from acting as an additional documentation cue that helps users understand a class, const functions are necessary if the program requires const instances of a class Now constancy isn't something you often want. After all, a const Customer is one who never places an order, never sets an address, never does anything much that is useful. But there are classes where const instances are meaningful. You can imagine uses for const Points:

```
const Point MinWindowSize(100.0, 100.0);
```

But there is a catch. The compiler is supposed to enforce constancy. So what is the compiler to do with code like:

```
// I need a bigger window
MinWindowSize.SetX(150.0);
// Test against window limits
if(xv < MinWindowSize.X()) ...
```

The second is a legitimate use of the variable MinWindowSize, the first changes it. The first should be disallowed, the second is permitted. The compiler can't know the rules unless you specify them. After all, the code for class Point may have been compiled years ago, all the compiler has to go on is the description in the header file. The compiler has to assume the worst. If you don't tell it that a member function leaves an object unchanged, the compiler must assume that it is changed. So, by default, a compiler refuses to let you use class member functions to manipulate const instances that class.

Inline Member Functions

Because the data in a class instance are protected, access functions have to be provided,

e.g.:

```
double Point::X() const
{
return fX;
}
```

Code needing the x-coordinate of a point must call this access function:

```
Point p1;
...
while(p1.X() > kMIN) { ...; p1.Offset(delta,
0.0); }
```

Calling a function simply to peek at a data member of an object can be a bit costly In praĉtice, it won't matter much except in cases where the access function is invoked in some deeply nested inner loop where every microsecond counts Now inline functions were invented in C++ to deal with situations where you want function semantics but you don't want to pay for function overheads. Inlines can be used to solve this particular version of the problem.

As always, the definition of an inline function has to have been read so that the compiler can expand a function call into actual code. Since classes are going to be declared in header files that get #included in all the code files that use class instances, the inline functions definitions must be in the header file.

The following is the preferred style:

```
#ifndef __MYGEOM__
#define __MYGEOM__
class Point {
public:
...
double X();
...
private:
...
double fX, fY, fR, fTheta;
};
other class declarations if any, e.g. class
Arc { };
inline double Point::X() { return fX; }
#endif
```

Any inline functions get defined at the end of the file. An alternative style is:

```
#ifndef __MYGEOM__
#define __MYGEOM__
class Point {
public:
...
double X() { return this->fX; }
...
```

```
private:
...
double fX, fY, fR, fTheta;
};
other class declarations if any, e.g. class
Arc { };
#endif
```

Here, the body of the inline function appears in the function declaration (note, an explicit `this->` qualifier on the data members is highly advisable when this style is used). The disadvantage of this style is that it makes the class declaration harder to read. Remember, your class declaration is going to be read by your colleagues. They want to know what your class can do, they don't really care how the work gets done. If you put the function definitions in the class declaration itself, you force them to look at the gory details. In contrast, your colleagues can simply ignore any inlines defined at the end of a header file, they know that these aren't really their concern.

EXAMPLE: BITMAPS (SETS)

The information retrieval example, illustrated one simple use of a bitmap in an actual application The bitmaps in that example used '1/0' bits to indicate whether a document contained a specific keyword. Really, the example illustrated a kind of "set". The bitmap for a document represented the "set of keywords" in that document. The system had a finite number of keywords, so there was a defined maximum set size. Each possible keyword was associated with a specific bit position in the set.

Such sets turn up quite often. So a "bit map" component is something that you might expect to "reuse" in many applications. Designing a general component for reuse is actually quite hard. Normally, you have a specific application in mind and the functionality that you identify is consequently biased to the needs of that application. When you later attempt to reuse the class, you find some changes and extensions are necessary. It has been suggested that a reusable class is typically created, and then reworked completely a couple of times before it becomes a really reusable component.

So, the class developed here may not exactly match the needs of your next application, but it should be a good starting point This example serves as an introduction to the design of a class. Remember a class is a C++ description of a particular type of component that will be used in programs Objects that are instances of the class will own some of the program's data and will provide all the services related to the owned data. The place to start designing a class is deciding what data its instances own and what services they provide What data does an individual bitmap own? Each instance of class `Bitmap` will have an array of unsigned long integers. There shouldn't be any other data members. To make things simple, we can have the `Bitmap` class use a fixed size array, with the size defined by a #define constant.

The next step is to decide what "services" a bitmap object should provide. You make up a list of useful functions. The list doesn't have to be complete, you can add further functionality later. Some useful services of a bitmap would be:

— Zeroing; reset all the bits to zero (the constructor function should call this, bit maps should start with all their bits set to 0).

— Set bit i; and Clear bit i; Need functions to set (make '1') and clear (make '0') a specified bit. This could be done by having separate set() and clear() functions, or a set_as() function that had two arguments - the bit number and the setting. Actually, it would probably be convenient if the class interface offered both forms because sometimes one form is more convenient than the other.

— Test bit i; Will often want to test the status of an individual bit.

— Flip bit i;

Change setting of a specified bit, if it was '1' it becomes '0' and vice versa.

— ReadFrom and WriteTo

Will want to transfer the data as a block of binary information.

— PrintOn

Produce a (semi)-readable printout of a bitmap as a series of hex values.

— Count

Get Bitmap to report how many bits it has set to '1'.

— Invert

Not clear whether this function would be that useful, but it might. The invert function would flip all the bits; all the '1's become '0's, all the '0's become '1's (the bitmap applies a "Not" operation to itself).

The next group of functions .combine two bitmaps to produce a third as a result Having a class instance as a function's result is just the same as having a struct as a result. As explained for structs, you must always consider whether this is wise. It can involve the use of lots of space on the stack and lots of copying operations. In this case it seems reasonable. Bitmap objects aren't that large and the function semantics are sensible.

— "And" with bit map "other"

Returns the bitmap that represents the And of the bitmap with a second bitmap.

— "Inclusive Or" with bitmap "other".

— "Exclusive Or" with bitmap "other".

and for consistency

— "Not"

Returns a bit map that is the inverse of this bitmap.

Finally, we should probably include an "Equals" function that checks equality with a second bitmap. The discussion of design based on top down functional decomposition favoured textual rather than diagrammatic representation.

The next stage in class design involves firming up the function prototypes, deciding on the arguments, return types, and const status. (There may not be much use for const Bitmaps, but you should still make the distinction between access functions that merely look at the data of a class member and modifying procedures that change data.) In general, it would also be necessary to produce pseudocode outlines for each function.

The prototypes become:

```
         Bitmap();

void     Zero(void);
void     SetBit(int bitnum);
void     ClearBit(int bitnum);
```

```
void     SetAs(int bitnum, int setting);
int      TestBit(int bitnum) const;
void     FlipBit(int bitnum);
void     ReadFrom(fstream& in);
void     WriteTo(fstream& out) const;
void     PrintOn(ostream& printer) const;
int      Count(void) const;
void     Invert(void);
Bitmap   And(const Bitmap& other) const;
Bitmap   Or(const Bitmap& other) const;
Bitmap   XOr(const Bitmap& other) const;
Bitmap   Not(void) const;
int      Equals(const Bitmap& other)
         const;
```

About the only point to note are the const `Bitmap&` arguments in functions like `And()`. We don't want to have `Bitmaps` passed by value (too much copying of data) so pass by reference is appropriate. The "And" operation does not affect the two bitmaps it combines, so the argument is const. The i/o functions take `fstream` reference arguments.

Only 0 and 1 values are appropriate for argument setting in function `SetAs()`. It would be possible to define an enumerated type for this, but that seems overkill. The coding can use 0 to mean 0 (reasonable) and non-zero to mean 1.

Implementation

The Bitmap class will be declared in a header file bitmap.h:

```
#ifndef __MYBITSCLASS__
#define __MYBITSCLASS__
// Code use iostream and fstream,
```

```
// #include these if necessary, fstream.h
// does a #include on iostream.h
#ifndef __FSTREAM_H
#include <fstream.h>
#endif
// Code assumes 32-bit unsigned long
 integers
#define MAXBITS 512
#define NUMWORDS 16
typedef unsigned long Bits;
class Bitmap {
public:
Bitmap();
   void     Zero(void);
   void     SetBit(int bitnum);
   void     ClearBit(int bitnum);
   void     SetAs(int bitnum, int
            setting);
   int      TestBit(int bitnum) const;
   void     FlipBit(int bitnum);
   void     ReadFrom(fstream& in);
   void     WriteTo(fstream& out) const;
   void     PrintOn(ostream& printer)
            const;
   int      Count(void) const;
   void     Invert(void);
   Bitmap   And(const Bitmap& other)
            const;
   Bitmap   Or(const Bitmap& other) const;
   Bitmap   XOr(const Bitmap& other)
            const;
   Bitmap   Not(void) const;
            int Equals(const Bitmap&
            other) const; private:
```

```
        Bits     fBits[NUMWORDS];
};
#endif
```

This header file has a # include on fstream.h. Attempts to compile a file including bitmap.h without fstream.h will fail when the compiler reaches the i/o functions. Since there is this dependency, fstream.h is # included (note the use of conditional compilation directives, if fstream.h has already been included, it isn't read a second time). There is no need to #include iostream.h; the fstream.h header already checks this.

The functions implementing the Bitmap concept are defined in bitmap.c:

```
#include "bitmap.h"

Bitmap::Bitmap()

{

Zero();

}

void Bitmap::Zero(void)

{

for(int i=0;i<NUMWORDS; i++)

fBits[i] = 0;

}
```

The constructor, `Bitmap::Bitmap()`, can use the `Zero()` member function to initialize a bitmap. Function `Zero()` just needs to loop zeroing out each array element.

```
void Bitmap::SetBit(int bitnum)
```

```
{
if((bitnum < 0) || (bitnum >= MAXBITS))
return;
int word = bitnum / 32;
int pos = bitnum % 32;
Bits mask = 1 << pos;
fBits[word] |= mask;
}
```

Function `ClearBit()` has to remove a particular bit. It identifies the array element with the bit. Then, it sets up a mask with the specified bit set. Next it complements the mask so that every bit except the specified bit is set. Finally, this mask is "Anded" with the array element; this preserves all bits except the one that was to be cleared

```
void Bitmap::ClearBit(int bitnum)
{
if((bitnum < 0) || (bitnum >= MAXBITS))
return;
int word = bitnum / 32;
int pos = bitnum % 32;
Bits mask = 1 << pos;
mask = ~mask;
fBits[word] &= mask;
}
```

Function `SetAs()` can rely on the implementation of `ClearBit()` and `SetBit()`:

```
void Bitmap::SetAs(int bitnum, int setting)
{
if(setting == 0)
ClearBit(bitnum);
else SetBit(bitnum);
}
```

Function `TestBit ()` uses the same mechanism for identifying the array element and bit and creating a mask with the chosen bit set. This mask is "Anded" with the array element. If the result is non-zero, the chosen bit must be set.

```
int Bitmap::TestBit(int bitnum) const
{
if((bitnum < 0) || (bitnum >= MAXBITS))
return 0;
int word = bitnum / 32;
int pos = bitnum % 32;
Bits mask = 1 << pos;
return (fBits[word] & mask);
}
```

Function `FlipBit()` uses an exclusive or operation to change the appropriate bit in the correct word:

```
void Bitmap::FlipBit(int bitnum)
{
if((bitnum < 0) || (bitnum >= MAXBITS))
return;
```

```
int word = bitnum / 32;
int pos = bitnum % 32;
Bits mask = 1 << pos;
fBits[word] ^= mask;
}
```

Functions `ReadFrom ()` and `WriteTo()` perform the binary transfers that copy the entire between file and memory:

```
void Bitmap::ReadFrom(fstream& in)
{
in.read(&fBits, sizeof(fBits));
}
void Bitmap::WriteTo(fstream& out) const
{
out.write(&fBits, sizeof(fBits));
}
```

These functions do not check for transfer errors. That can be done in the calling environment. When coding class `Bitmap`, you don't know what should be done if a transfer fails. (Your IDE's version of the iostream library, and its compiler, may differ slightly; the calls to read and write may need "(`char*`)" inserted before `&fBits`.)

The files produced using `WriteTo()` are unreadable by humans because they contain the "raw" binary data. Function `PrintOn()` produces a readable output:

```
void Bitmap::PrintOn(ostream& printer)
const
```

```
{
long savedformat = printer.flags();
printer.setf(ios::showbase);
printer.setf(ios::hex,ios::basefield);
for(int i = 0; i <NUMWORDS; i++) {
printer.width(12);
printer << fBits[i];
if((i % 4) == 3) cout << endl;
}
printer.flags(savedformat);
}
```

Function `PrintOn ()` has to change the output stream so that numbers are printed in hex. It would be somewhat rude to leave the output stream in the changed state! So `PrintOn ()` first uses the `flags ()` member function of ostream to get the current format information. Before returning, `PrintOn ()` uses another overloaded version of the `flags ()` function to set the format controls back to their original state.

```
int Bitmap::Count(void) const
{
int count = 0;
for(int n=0; n < NUMWORDS; n++) {
Bits x = fBits[n];
int j = 1;
for(int i=0;i<32;i++) {
```

```
if(x & j)
count++;
j = j << 1;
}
}
return count;
}
```

The `Count ()` function uses a double loop, the outer loop steps through the array elements, the inner loop checks bits in the current element. It might be worth changing the code so that the inner loop was represented as a separate `CountBitsInElement()` function. This would be a private member function of class Bitmap Functions `Invert()`, `Not ()` and `Equals ()` all have similar loops that check, change, or copy and change successive array elements from `fBits`:

```
void Bitmap::Invert(void)
{
for(int i=0; i < NUMWORDS; i++)
fBits[i] = ~fBits[i];
}
Bitmap Bitmap:: Not(void) const
{
Bitmap b;
for(int i = 0; i < NUMWORDS; i++)
b.fBits[i] = ~this->fBits[i];
return b;
```

```
}

int Bitmap::Equals(const Bitmap& other)
const

{

for(int I = 0; I < NUMWORDS; i++)

if(this->fBits[I] != other.fBits[i]) return
0;

return 1;

}
```

Note the explicit use of the `this->` qualifier in `Not()` and `Equals()`. These functions manipulate more than one `Bitmap`, and hence more than one `fBits` array. There are the `fBits` data member of the object executing the function, and that of some second object. The `this->` qualifier isn't needed but sometimes it makes things clearer You will also note that the `Bitmap` object that is performing the `Equals ()` operation is looking at the fBits data member of the second `Bitmap (other)`. What about the "walls" around `other's` data?

Classes basically define families of objects and there are no secrets within families An object executing code of a member function of the class is permitted to look in the private data areas of any other object of that class. The functions `And()`, `Or()`, and `XOr()` are very similar in coding. The only difference is the operator used to combine array elements:

```
Bitmap Bitmap::And(const Bitmap& other)
const

{

Bitmap b;
```

```
for(int i = 0; i < NUMWORDS; i++)
b.fBits[i] = this->fBits[i] &
other.fBits[i];
return b;
}
Bitmap Bitmap::Or(const Bitmap& other)
const
{
Bitmap b;
for(int i = 0; i < NUMWORDS; i++)
b.fBits[i] = this->fBits[i] |
other.fBits[i];
return b;
}
Bitmap Bitmap::XOr(const Bitmap& other)
const
{
Bitmap b;
for(int i = 0; i < NUMWORDS; i++)
b.fBits[i] = this->fBits[i] ^
other.fBits[i];
return b;
}
```

It isn't sufficient to write the class, you must also test it! The test program should automatically exercise all aspects of the class. This test program becomes part of the class documentation. It has to be available to other programmers who may need to extend or modify the existing class and who will need to retest the code after their modifications.

The test program for class Bitmap is:

```
int main()
{
Test1();
Test2();
Test3();
return EXIT_SUCCESS;
}
```

There are three Test functions (and an auxiliary function). As the names imply, the functions were developed and implemented in sequence. Basic operations were checked out using `Test1 ()` before the code of `Test2 ()` and `Test3 ()` was implemented. The first test function checks out simple aspects like setting and clearing bits and getting a `Bitmap` printed:

```
void Test1()
{
// Try setting some bits and just printing
   the
// resulting Bitmap
int somebits[] = { 0, 3, 4, 6, 9, 14,
                   21, 31,32, 40, 48, 56,
                   64, 91, 92, 93, 94, 95,
                   500, 501
                                  };
int n = sizeof(somebits) / sizeof(int);
Bitmap b1;
```

```
SetBits(b1, somebits, n);
cout << "Test 1" << endl;
cout << "b1:" << endl;
b1.PrintOn(cout);
cout << "Number of bits set in b1 is "
        << b1.Count()
        << endl;
cout << "(that should have said " << n
        << ")" << endl;
if(b1.TestBit(20)) cout << "Strange I didn't
think I set bit 20" << endl;
 if(!b1.TestBit(3)) cout << "Something
    just ate my bitmap" << endl;
    b1.Invert();
    cout << "Look at b1, it's flipped" <<
    endl;
 b1.PrintOn(cout);
 b1.Zero();
    SetBits(b1, somebits, n);
    cout << "sanity restored" << endl;
    b1.ClearBit(4);
    b1.FlipBit(6);
    b1.FlipBit(7);
    cout << "Check for three small changes:"
    << endl;
    b1.PrintOn(cout);
    }
```

An auxiliary function `SetBits()` was defined to make it easier to set several bits:

```
  void SetBits(Bitmap& theBitmap, int
bitstoset[], int num)

  {

  for(int i=0; i<num; i++) {
```

```
   int b = bitstoset[i];
   theBitmap.SetBit(b);
   }
   }
```

Function `Test2()` checks the transfers to/from files, and also the `Equals()` function:

```
void Test2()
   {
   int somebits[] = { 0, 1, 2, 3, 5, 7, 11,
13,
   17, 19, 23, 29, 31, 37,
   41, 47
   };
   int n = sizeof(somebits) / sizeof(int);
   Bitmap b1;
   SetBits(b1, somebits, n);
   fstream tempout("tempbits", ios::out);
   if(!tempout.good()) {
   cout << "Sorry, Couldn't open temporary
output file" << endl; exit(1);
   }
   b1.WriteTo(tempout);
   if(!tempout.good()) {
   cout << "Seem to have had problems writing
to file"
```

```
<< endl;
exit(1);
}
tempout.close();
Bitmap b2;
fstream tempin("tempbits", ios::in |
ios::nocreate);
if(!tempin.good()) {
cout << "Sorry, couldn't open temp file
with"
" the bits" << endl; exit(1);
}
b2.ReadFrom(tempin);
if(!tempin.good()) {
cout << "Seem to have had problems reading
from"
" file" << endl;
exit(1);
}
tempin.close();
cout << "I wrote the bitmap :" << endl;
b1.PrintOn(cout);
cout << "I read the bitmap : " << endl;
b2.PrintOn(cout);
if(b1.Equals(b2)) cout << "so i got as
good as i gave" << endl; else cout << "which
is sad" << endl;
```

```
}
```

The final function checks whether the implementations of `And()`,`Or()`,`XOr()` and `Not()` are mutually consistent. (It doesn't actually check whether they are right, just that they are consistent). It relies on relationships like: "A Or B" is the same as "Not (Not A And Not B)"

```
void Test3()
   {
   int somebits[] = {
   2, 4, 6, 8, 16,
   33, 35, 37, 39, 41, 43, 45, 47, 49, 51,
53, 55,
   68, 74, 80, 86,
   102, 112, 122, 132,
   145, 154, 415, 451
   };
   int n = sizeof(somebits) / sizeof(int);
   Bitmap b1;
   SetBits(b1, somebits, n);
   int otherbits[] = {
   2, 3, 6, 9, 16,
   23, 25, 27, 49, 52, 63, 75, 87, 99,
   102, 113, 132, 143,
   145, 241, 246, 362, 408, 422, 428, 429,
500, 508
   };
```

```
int m = sizeof(otherbits) / sizeof(int);
Bitmap b2;
SetBits(b2, otherbits, m);
Bitmap b3 = b1.Or(b2);
Check equality
Evaluate Or directly
Bitmap b4 = b1.Not();
Bitmap b5 = b2.Not();
Bitmap b6 = b4.And(b5);
b6.Invert();
if(b6.Equals(b3)) cout << "The ands, ors
and nots are " "consistent" << endl;
else cout << "back to the drawing board"
<< endl;
b3 = b1.XOr(b2);
b4 = b1.And(b2);
b5 = b4.Not();
b6 = b1.Or(b2);
b6 = b6.And(b5);
if(b3.Equals(b6)) cout << "XOr kd" << endl;
else cout << "XOr what?" << endl;
}
```

A class isn't complete until you have written a testing program and checked it out. Class `Bitmap` passed these tests. It may not be perfect but it appears useable.

2

Computer Use of Teachers

Teacher professional development increasingly recognizes the importance of the expertise of practicing teachers and of teachers learning from and with one another. These new roles and support structures for teachers can work together to establish a professional culture in schools-a culture of collaboration rather than a culture of individualism. This collaborative approach to professional leadership is viewed as central to school change. The isolation and silence of teachers in the discourses on teaching and learning can be seen as a "protective response to subordination".

Teachers, without a sense of agency or authority beyond the classroom, engage in a form of "private practice" behind closed doors. Closed classroom doors open concerns about maintaining high standards for both teaching and learning. This research focuses on how these teachers are similar and different from the group of teacher leaders. In contrast to this form of private practice, teacher leaders and professionals engage in collaborative dialog about teaching and learning with a belief that "part of being a teacher involves grappling with and collectively confronting the contradictory demands of the educational system,". The shift from privacy and self-reliance to collaboration and experimentation or continuous improvement represents a significant shift in values. Institutional factors like school culture and organizational practices help shape the way teachers view their role in the school. Teacher leaders view their relationship to other educators within and beyond the school as an important determinant of the quality of student learning in the classroom. We begin this paper with a review of the literature in two areas:

(1) the rationale for our choice of teacher leadership dimensions; and

(2) a brief discussion of our choice of dimensions for discussing school philosophy, practice and computer use.

Teacher Leadership Dimensions

Collaborative forms of professional development exist at the school site and beyond the school and include participation in peer review groups, teacher networks, and partnerships with universities and organizations, and programs. They involve teachers in national, state, and local school and curriculum reform activities.

Teacher Leadership in School

Teacher leaders improve classroom practice by engaging other teachers in critical reflection on their experiences and sharing classroom experiences with other teachers in formal and informal ways.

Informal Discussions

Teachers working together to explore dimensions of teaching and learning, creating school improvement plans, and developing school curriculum are directly linked to effective schools. Some found that successful teacher school networks unite members who share interests and concerns around a common goal that the participants themselves believe to be important. Little underscores the importance of a school culture "teachers valued and participated in norms of collegiality and continuous improvement." Strong networks also provide participants with an opportunity to interact in a non-threatening environment where both teaching and learning occur simultaneously.

Teacher Mentoring and Classroom Visits

Teacher mentoring is a school reform strategy that recognizes and rewards the talent and expertise of master teachers. Teacher leaders work with in one-to-one relationships with colleagues as peer mentors, providing information and feedback on the implementation of a new program or on a promising instructional strategy. In this role, teachers are able to use their extensive knowledge of teaching in specific school contexts to help colleagues who may be new to teaching or new to the school. This peer teaching and collaboration approach encourages the development of local expertise.

Opportunities to observe others, to model desired behaviors, to benefit from coaching by colleagues, and to receive meaningful feedback on their progress help create a culture of collaboration. While recognizing that some mentoring programs can be conservative in nature with experts transmitting a skill-based culture to a new generation of teachers, for many these programs are viewed as catalysts for transformational change in school culture. Because mentoring programs are based on teachers working together, and supporting one another, they can create a school culture of collaboration. However, the development of these programs may be an important dimension with mandated mentoring programs leading to "contrived collegiality" rather than to a culture of collaboration.

Informal Communications

Professionally engaged teachers see teaching as a process of continual, reflective inquiry and the exchange of ideas with their peers leading to the development of a shared technical language and a shared knowledge base. They value opportunities to share their expertise with colleagues beyond their schools. Out-of-school experiences-collaborations with formal and informal networks, partnerships with community groups, and involvement in district, state, national and international education activities-expand teachers' understanding of policy and practice in ways that are sometimes unavailable in school. The recent availability of email and Internet access encourages informal professional and leadership opportunities.

Professional Development Opportunities

Teachers are often required to attend workshops given by "outside experts' in teaching and learning while their knowledge-gained from years of practice-is undervalued. This encourages a view of "teaching as technical, learning as packaged, and teachers as passive recipients of "objective research." School district and organizational meetings provide an avenue for teachers to share their ideas beyond the school. Teachers can voice their need for professional development that extends far beyond the one-shot workshop toward fulfilling their expressed need for opportunities to learn how to question, analyze, and change instruction to teach challenging content development. Darling-Hammond and McLaughlin argue for new forms of staff development which provide "occasions for teachers to reflect critically on their practice and to fashion new knowledge and beliefs about content, pedagogy, and learners."

The goal is to engage teachers in studying specific aspects of practice, comparing ideas on implementation, and seeking new ideas or programs. Increasingly teachers are serving as instructors and participants in new forms of professional development that go beyond those that impart research results to engaging teachers in active programs that involve continual partnerships. These district meetings also provide teachers with the opportunity to review curriculum plans, instructional programs and student assessment practices. As teachers identify more and more professional development capacity within their school, they become less dependent on traditional forms of professional development.

Teacher leaders often attend conferences and workshops as presenters rather than participants. Some teachers become involved in trainer of trainers programs where their presentation is more likely to be constrained within a model or program that supports teachers teaching teachers. But often teacher leaders create presentations about their own innovations. To do this well, teachers need to place themselves at a distance and view their work from the perspectives of their peers. The process of extracting elements of their practice and conceptualizing it for others creates the distributive expertise that is basic to a learning community. Other leadership opportunities are available by formal relationships with universities where teacher leaders spend some of their time teaching either pre-service or in-service teachers. Increasingly, there is a call for professional development schools where expert teachers serve as instructional leaders for new teachers. Teaching in professional development schools revitalizes and veteran teachers for their contribution to the education beyond their classroom teaching.

In communities around the country, teachers-either alone or in groups-are gathering information, analyzing experiences and events, and writing about the issues and problems they confront in schools and classrooms. By publishing their work, teacher leaders share their ideas and strategies with the larger profession. There are at least four reasons for why publishing for teachers is so important. The first is that the process of knowledge construction involves critical thinking and reflection that leads to deeper knowledge.

The second is the experience can lead to a deeper understanding of how to guide novice writers. Third, teachers who are authors are more likely to be participants in a academic discourse closing the gap between teaching and research. Fourth, teacher knowledge on how programmatic and organizational changes might be effective in their school or districts can be a valuable resource for school reform.

Dimensions of Teaching Philosophy, Practice, and Computer Use

To understand how teacher leaders differ from other teachers, we examine their philosophy, practice and use of computer technology in terms of current theories of teaching and learning. Teachers today are expected to prepare all students to reach significantly higher academic standards than have previously been attempted in this country. The student populations that teachers are asked to work with are diverse and have complex learning needs. The range of methods and approaches and the theories of teaching and learning demand extensive intellectual preparation and continual learning on the part of teachers. The rapid speed of technological development brings new computer mediated tools to the classroom door each year. Teachers have to make continual decisions about how to best utilize these tools in teaching, learning and assessment.

School reform programs are efforts to solve a range of educational problems, however, our examination of the discourse of reform suggests that many of them either explicitly or implicitly derive from theories of learning that can be grouped under the rubric of constructivism. These include cognitive constructivism, inquiry learning theories, sociohistorical activity theories, social constructivism, meta-cognitive theories, and recent brainbased learning.

These constructivist-compatible instructional activities are quite distinct from a cultural or knowledge transmission view of learning that emphasizes teacher-centered whole-class explanation and closely scripted student seatwork. This same distinction is used to understand teacher responses about their classroom practices. Classroom teachers who define instruction as the transmission of knowledge have students learn concepts and skills through listening, copying text, and practicing sets of similar problems.

Classroom teachers who define instruction as the co-construction of knowledge focus on project activities that expect students to display understanding, interpretation, and original thought. The questions about practices asked teachers to describe classroom activities in a current on-going classroom unit. The questions were posed so that teachers frequently had to make a choice among options that were closer to one of these two contrasting approaches to classroom instruction.

Computers can be defined in similar ways to convey information, for practicing responses or for tutorials. These are all knowledge transmission uses. Computers can also be used for student inquiry and presentation of students' work. These are coconstruction uses.

Source of Data, Sampling, and Weighting

The study of teacher professionalism, pedagogy, and computer use is drawn from data collected in 1998 as part of a national survey. "Teaching, Learning, and Computing-1998" surveyed teachers from a national probability sample of schools-898 schools stratified by school level (elementary, middle, high school). It also includes a sample of 718 schools selected either because of the presence of substantial computer technology in the school or because of the involvement of at least one teacher, if not the whole school, in instructional reform activities. In both the probability sample of schools and the specially selected schools (we refer to the latter as the "purposive" sample), most of the teachers were selected using probability sampling methods from among all teachers of grades 4-12.

About one-sixth of the teachers were selected because of their participation in reform programs or their principal's designation of them as exemplary users of constructivist/ cognitive approaches.3 Seventy-five percent of schools (N=1215) participated to the point of rostering their teachers for sampling. Among the teachers sampled or selected with certainty, 4,083 provided completed useable surveys, 67% of those rostered and sampled. This includes 2,251 teachers from the probability sample, 1,236 from reform-involved schools, and 596 from the high technology-presence schools. The analysis for this paper combines the probability and the purposive sample in such a way as to take account of the sampling weights of different schools and different teachers in the same school. We also maintain the balance in total numbers between the probability sample (55% of the total sample) and the purposive sample.

Defining Teacher Leaders

We define Teacher Leaders as teachers in our sample who were actively engaged with their peers both at their own school and beyond their school and who indicated that they were engaged in mentoring other teachers, presenting at workshops, university teaching, or publishing. At the other end of our continuum were those teachers who we call Private Practice Teachers. Those were teachers who, by indicating relatively little professional interaction with peers, could be inferred were either implementing mandated policies or found themselves to be both self-sufficient in their teaching practice and uninterested in assisting others in their field.

We also labeled teachers in two intermediate categories: Teacher Professionals were closer to Teacher Leaders, while Interactive Teachers were closer to Private Practice Teachers. The placement of teachers into these categories was determined by three multi-part survey questions, each of which was used to form an index which in turn contributed to the overall measure of professional engagement from which the four categories were formed. Within-School Teacher Interaction. From the first question set, we formed an index of "Within-School Teacher Interaction." This was the average frequency that the teacher reported having six types of interactions with other teachers at their own school. Those interactions included discussions about teaching methods, project ideas, subject-matter issues, and technology as well as reports of informal observations of another or ones own teaching. Informal interactions averaging halfway between "several per month" and "one to three times per week" was one of the three criteria used to define Teacher Leaders. To be a Teacher Professional, an average answer of "several per month" was needed.

Beyond-School Teacher Contact. A second survey question dealt with similar interactions-but with teachers at other schools. "Beyond-School Teacher Contact" was defined as how many of the following three criteria the teachers met: attending workshops with teachers from other schools at least 3 times since September; going to 3 or more committee meetings with teachers from other schools; and using electronic mail with teachers at other schools at least a half-dozen times. To be considered a Teacher Leader, two of these criteria needed to be met; Teacher Professionals had to meet only one of these criteria of Beyond-School Teacher Contact.

Teachers completed surveys between March and June of 1998.Leadership. The third survey question asked about the teacher's involvement over the past three years in six types of leadership activities within the profession, including mentoring other teachers (2 measures), giving workshop presentations (2 measures), teaching college-level courses, and publishing. The number among these six activities reported by the teacher formed the teacher's "Leadership Activity" score. Teacher Leaders engaged in at least three of these six activities; Teacher Professionals did at least two.

Teacher Leaders and Teacher Professionals had to meet standards deriving from each of the three survey questions. The standards for Teacher Leaders were simply more rigorous. Among those who did not meet standards on within-school interactions, between-school contacts, and leadership activities, we distinguished between teachers who were generally interactive with other teachers, having at least a mean score on an index combining answers to all three survey questions, from those who had a score below the mean, overall. The former we titled Interactive Teachers; the latter, Private Practice Teachers. Although this paper focuses on the Teacher Leaders, we present data on all four groups to provide a context for understanding the survey responses of the Teacher Leaders.

Pedagogy: Direct Instruction vs. Knowledge Construction

To measure instructional practice, teachers were asked a set of questions that focused on how frequently they employed specific instructional strategies in the one class in which they felt most accomplished as a teacher. An index was constructed based on the mean scores of 27 item prompts from five survey questions: Methods used to introduce the current unit to the class included introductory drills, small group discussions, making conjectures, and raising truly problematic questions. The last three were coded in the direction of "Knowledge Construction." Reasons given for asking students questions included eliciting student opinion, getting students to justify their reasoning, and relating issues to students' experiences.

How the most recent five hours of class time had been spent, including teacher-led whole-class discussion (coded

"Direct Instruction"), student presentations and student led discussion, and student small group work. Frequency of various types of assignments and class activities included individual seatwork ("direct instruction"), hands-on activities, weeklong projects, journalwriting, planning classroom activities, problem-solving in small groups, working on problems with no obvious method for solving, explaining their reasoning by writing, holding formal debates, designing their own problems to solve, small group discussions of procedures for solving problems, doing oral or written reflection on their own work, tasks involving multiple representations of the same idea, making a product to be used by someone else, demonstrating work to an audience (other than their class or parents), and undertaking tasks without clear correct answers.

The alpha reliability for this index was .86. For this paper, the index was divided roughly into quartiles, with teachers in the lowest quartile classified as "direct instructionoriented" and those in the highest quartile as "knowledge construction-oriented" in terms of pedagogy.

EDUCATIONAL PHILOSOPHY

Teacher beliefs about good practice-their educational philosophy-is a control variable in the main analysis. Beliefs about teaching that derive from constructivist learning theory represent a potential for implementing a constructivistcompatible teaching practice. Yet, it is well understood that implementing many of these practices is hard work. One question we address in this paper is whether leaders are more able to implement a constructivist pedagogy than are other teachers, even when they hold essentially similar teaching philosophies. Our measure of teaching philosophy comes from three survey questions, incorporating individual prompts. In one question, teachers were asked to compare two teachers' approaches to classroom discussion, one approach representing traditional teacher-directed questioning based on prior reading, the other representing teacher-led discussion that provoked questions from the students themselves which the teacher then reflected back to them for further research. A second set of questions presented paired comparisons of contrasting teaching philosophies, each item presented as a hypothetical personal statement of beliefs. The third question involved a set of six agree vs. disagree statements (6-point scales) including statements about the importance of background knowledge as a rationale for , the value of building instruction around problems with "clear, correct answers" and ideas "that most students can grasp quickly," and the need to postpone "meaningful learning" until basic skills have been acquired.

An index was created by taking the mean of these prompts, after equalizing item standard deviations (effectively creating standard scores for items). The alpha reliability for this index was .84.

Computer Use

Teacher involvement in using computers involves having students use a variety of software as part of their classroom instructional practice as well as using computers for their own professional work. In addition, a strong computer-use practice would seem to involve reasonably substantial expertise in using basic computer applications and having adequate resources available for professional and student use. The survey contained several measures of computer access and use that we placed into a broader operational definition of teacher involvement with computers:

1) The extent to which teachers had students use each of 10 different types of software (the Web, spreadsheets and databases, multimedia authoring software, word processing, games for practicing skills, simulations, presentation software, e-mail, programs for printing graphics, and CD-ROM reference software)
2) The variety of ways they themselves used computers professionally (e.g., corresponding with parents, getting information or pictures for the Web for use in lessons, and exchanging computer files with other teachers)
3) The extent of their technical expertise (e.g., knowing how to make and present a slide show, develop a multimedia document, create a new database, etc.)
4) Their experience and felt expertise with Windows and Macintosh platforms
5) How many computers they had in their classroom
6) The variety of other technology resources which their schools gave them access to (e.g., classroom telephone, easy access to a fax machine, Internet access and electronic mail from their classroom, access to the school's computer network from home)
7) How long they had had a home computer and Internet access
8) Whether their students had ever used computers for complex, integrative projects (several examples shown and asked about)
9) The extent that their use of computers had increased in several ways over the past five years (e.g., for class preparation, for student projects)

Factor analysis of all of the different indicators of computer use produced three dimensions of teacher computer involvement, which we labeled "Student Tool Use," "Frequent (relatively simple) Uses," and "Teacher Use and Expertise." These three dimensions were combined, and, using a judgmental process, cutoff points were chosen that, in combination, selected 10% of all teachers as Highly Active Computer Users (Computer education teachers and business education teachers were excluded from the factor analysis and subsequent categorizations because computer use was essentially defined as essential elements of their courses.) Between 9% and 10% of teachers of each school level passed these cutoff points to be designated as Highly Active Computer Users. Teachers of most subject-areas were in the range of 9% to 12%, with only foreign language (3%) and mathematics teachers (4%) below that point and vocational education teachers (16%) above.

Our contrast of Teacher Leaders with other categories of teacher Professional Engagement will be reported in three major sections, (1) descriptions of personal and educational backgrounds, teaching responsibilities, and participation in staff development activities (2) teaching philosophies related to pedagogical practices and (3) computer use. Throughout, we contrast the Teacher Leaders with the other categories of teacher professional engagement.

Professional and Personal Characteristics

We use personal and professional characteristics including information on teachers' educational background experiences and current participation in learning to provide an image of Teacher Leaders.

Personal Characteristics and Teaching Experience

Teacher Leaders, on the average, are about 5 years older and have had 5 years more teaching experience than the other teachers in the sample. While it makes sense that veteran teachers should be providing leadership, this finding runs contrary to assertions often made about teachers, such as that older teachers, educated at a time when teaching was seen as a more solitary activity, might be less likely to be involved in professional activities. Clearly, that is not the case. In the overall sample, 66% of the respondents were female. Private Practice Teachers were 65% female which is very similar. However the Teacher Leaders were more likely to be female with 74% female.

Educational Background

The Teacher Leaders came from more selective schools, maintained higher grade point averages, and were more likely to have graduate degrees than the rest of the teachers in the sample. When we combine the educational background information into an index, and compare Teacher Leaders' to the total sample, their average "Educational Investment" places them in 69th percentile nationally. Teacher Professionals are also more educated than typical teachers in the sample (60th percentile). The Private Practice Teachers are, in contrast, less well educated (45th percentile). Although there are likely to be many very good teachers who are isolated in their classrooms, this data suggests that those who close the door are teachers with less academic preparation than those who are engage in professional activities.

Teaching Responsibilites

Teacher Leaders and Teacher Professionals were distributed proportionally across subject areas and grade levels in the national probability sample-selected to represent the nation -with one exception: Proportionately more computer education teachers were included in these two categories of the more professionally engaged teachers. Thus, it appears that teachers who teach computer classes, as a whole, are more engaged in a collaborative culture than teachers from other subject areas.

The Teacher Leaders and Professionals who were identified from the purposive sample- the reform programs schools and schools with very high levels of technology- showed more variation by subject area. These schools appear to have proportionally more professional leadership in interdisciplinary subjects, in applied secondary subjects, and in elementary self-contained classrooms.

Teacher Leaders spend, on the average, 6 more days than other teachers in staff development activities. If we contrast Teacher Leaders with those teachers who are isolated in their classrooms, the Teacher Leaders are spending twice as much time in professional development activities. When looking at the content of these sessions, the Teacher Leaders were more likely to be engaged in professional development activities which focused on technology and instructional strategies than the teachers in the other groups.

Philosophy and Pedagogy and Professional Engagement

Using the complex of questions that formed our Philosophy Index, we arranged the teachers by quartiles from those who see the aim of education as knowledge transmission to those who hold that knowledge construction is the basic aim. Only 3% of the Teacher Leaders fall in the knowledge transmission quartile compared to 32% of the Private Practice Teachers, while 58% define their overall goals in educational as consistent with a constructivist philosophy (compared to only 20% of Private Practice Teachers).

The private practice

Teachers are the only group to have a higher percent of teachers who hold the more traditional views of knowledge transmission than hold knowledge construction viewpoints. However, it is important to remember that Private Practice Teachers are also the largest group in the sample and represent half of the teaching population.

We asked teachers to select one class period in which they were most satisfied with their teaching, the one in which they felt that they were closest to accomplishing their educational goals. All the questions about teacher pedagogy (i.e., their actual teaching practice) were about this particular class. The items from the Pedagogy Index were divided into quartiles, similar to how the Philosophy Index was handled.

A series of exploratory factor analyses of the 27 survey prompts that comprised the Pedagogy Index revealed that the items can be reasonably assigned to four different subcomponents: (1) the use of student projects; (2) small group work; (3) tasks involving cognitive challenge; and (4) presence or absence of direct instruction. Teacher Leaders differ most from the other three categories of teachers on items measuring student project work, where they are nearly one full standard deviation above the mean for all teachers in the TLC sample.

Subject-matter teaching responsibilities was a principal determinant of how constructivist a teacher appears to be, both in philosophy and pedagogy. However, within each group of subject-matter specialists, Teacher Leaders and Teacher Professionals are far more constructivist in practice than Interactive Teachers or Private Practice Teachers. There are three measures-the overall Pedagogy Index and sub-indices for two of its primary components-Projects and Cognitive Challenge. Because we have seen that Teacher Leaders and Professionals have much more constructivist-oriented teaching philosophies than Private Practice Teachers, it is not clear whether the differences in pedagogy. However, implementing a constructivist philosophy is quite difficult. If Teacher Leaders are actually more successful teachers (that is, not only more professionally engaged, but actually more able to implement difficult teaching practices), we would need to control on philosophy in order to see whether the average Teacher Leader's pedagogy is more constructivist than other teachers who happen to hold similarly constructivist teaching philosophies as the Teacher Leader.

Controlling for philosophy makes it possible for us to match Teacher Leaders with other teachers in the sample who expressed similar philosophical beliefs about the best teaching and learning strategies. We then look at how they describe their classroom practices to see if they employ the strategies they believe are most effective in similar ways. We find that teacher leaders as well as teacher professionals were more likely to have constructivist pedagogy even when philosophy was controlled. Moreover, this was true for every subject-area separately.

The difference between Leaders/Professionals and Private Practice Teachers in terms of constructivist practice was greatest in social studies, where it reached nearly a full standard deviation; and it was smallest among science teachers, although even there it was more than one-half a standard deviation. Thus, it appears from these results that Teacher Leaders and Professionals are more successful in implementing their educational beliefs in the classroom.

There are a number of possible explanations for this. One is that with their better educational preparation and their more regular participation in intellectual exchanges with adults, they have learned the skills and strategies that make this translation possible. It is also possible that it is, in some ways, a reflection of their greater institutional power. That is, their identification as mentor teachers, conference presenters, or university instructors has given them more institutional power to enact their views of good education. They are less subject to the will of administrators pressured by parents and school boards to demonstrate student learning in terms of higher test scores.

Professional engagement and computer use

In this final section, we compare the frequency of computer use as well as differences in computer use by teachers who are more and less professionally engaged. Our principal focus is on instructional use by students during class time-how frequently teachers give students the opportunity to use computers, what types of software they have students use, and what their objectives for student computer use are. In addition, we employ a more comprehensive measure of teacher involvement with computers, one that incorporates teacher professional uses and their expertise. With this more comprehensive measure, we examine differences among the teacher leaders and teacher professionals between those who are highly active computer users and those for whom computers play a less central role in their teaching lives. In all of these comparisons, we are trying to understand the role that computer use plays with respect to the constructivist orientation of Teacher Leaders. Does computer use shape beliefs and practices or is it shaped by teachers' beliefs and practices?

PROFESSIONAL ENGAGEMENT AND COMPUTER USE

In nearly every subject-area of instruction, teacher leaders and teacher professionals are more likely to have their students use computers on a regular basis during class time than are Private Practice Teachers. For most subjects, they are also more likely than "Interactive Teachers" (the intermediate category of Professional Engagement) to give students regular (i.e., weekly) computer activities. The differences for the other academic subjects are smaller, but Professionally Engaged English teachers are half-again as likely as Interactive English Teachers to assign computer work on a frequent basis. Professionally Engaged Teachers use every type of software more than Private Practice Teachers. Even when only computer-assigning teachers are considered, the greater the level of professional engagement, the more frequently students of that teacher use a given type of software. Among computer-assigning teachers, students of Teacher Leaders average about 3.5 lessons using the Web while students of Private Practice Teachers average 1.75 lessons, a ratio of two to one.

The greatest differences between Professionally Engaged Teachers and Private Practice Teachers in how frequently they have students use software is for electronic mail, multimedia authoring software, and presentation software. Those types of software are used primarily to communicate with other people and to produce products for an audience-activities closely associated with constructivist pedagogy. Those findings about which types of software most distinguish Professionally Engaged Teachers and Private Practice Teachers are confirmed by findings concerning the three "objectives" for students' computer use which they felt were most important in their own teaching. Frequent student use of constructivist software like multimedia authoring programs is one indicator of a sophisticated computer-using teacher-a teacher who has substantial computer competence.

Our comprehensive measure of teacher computer involvement incorporates frequent use of diverse software along with other measures of professional utilization and computer expertise. Overall, 10% of our sample's teachers passed the factor-analysis-derived criteria for being a highly active computer user. One of the most remarkable findings in this analysis is that Teacher Leaders were 10 times as likely as Private Practice Teachers to be designated a Highly Active Computer User. Forty percent of Teacher Leaders were compared to only 4% of Private Practice Teachers. About one-fourth of Teacher Professionals were Highly Active, six times as many as among Private Practice Teachers. Of all of the dimensions of background, teaching responsibility, teaching philosophy, and teaching practice on which we have compared teachers in terms of their professional engagement, from Teacher Leaders to Private Practice Teachers, none of them has produced differences on the order of magnitude of this measure of Highly Active Computer Use. Of the three component factors comprising the overall Teacher Computer Involvement index, Teacher Leaders are most different from other teachers in having students use "tool" software (mean z-score of +.88), and least different from other teachers in terms of frequent use of simple software (still more than one-half standard deviation higher than average, z=+.52). On Professional Computer Uses and Teacher Computer Expertise, their superiority was extremely high (+.67), but not as high as on Student Tool Uses.

Our results have demonstrated so far that, as a group, teachers who are professionally oriented-that is, who are involved in the teaching lives of their peers both at their own school and elsewhere-are much more likely than other teachers to be constructivists in beliefs, practice and computer use. Their objectives for using computers in their teaching are consistent with constructivist teaching philosophies, and in the last section, we demonstrated that they are more likely be Highly Active Computer Users overall. However, not all Teacher Leaders are constructivists and not all Teacher Leaders are active users of computers in their teaching. Are there systematic patterns within the group of teachers identified as professionally engaged? Do computer-active Teacher Leaders and Teacher Leaders who don't use computers very much in their practice themselves differ in terms of their educational backgrounds, teaching philosophies and practices, and in how they use computers (when they do use them)? In other words, are the relatively few Leaders who are transmission-oriented in their teaching also those who don't use computers very much or is there a substantial group of Teacher Leaders who are as constructivist as the others, but who choose not to use computers in their practice? First, it should be noted that professionally engaged teachers who are highly active computer users and their similarly-involved peers who do use computers less (or not at all) are fairly similar in terms of personal background characteristics. The two groups have identical average years of teaching experience and similar overall levels of educational investment.

Second, when examining the relationship between pedagogy and computer use across teachers in different subject areas, it is important to control on subject matter taught. This is because teachers of some subjects are more likely to be Highly Active Computer Users than others (i.e., vocational education more than math teachers), and teachers of those same subjects are more likely to be constructivist in practice. To do this analysis, we employed "within-subject-matter z-scores" to measure aspects of teaching philosophy and practice. These are standardized scores where the mean value for teachers of each subject is set to zero (with a standard deviation of 1.0), so we can look at differences, say between Highly Active Computer Users and other teachers, without worrying that one group may contain teachers of subjects with a greater propensity to be constructivist.

The difference in pedagogy is true even when controlling on philosophy-i.e., among professionally-involved teachers in the same subject-areas and with similar teaching philosophies, the Highly Active Computer Users are more constructivist in practice than the ones who use computers less. Most of the differences between highly active computer users and others are at least one-fourth of a standard deviation. The two computer use categories (Highly Active vs. all others) differ in philosophy and pedagogy nearly as much as do the two categories of Professional Engagement-Teacher Professionals and Teacher Leaders.

Overall, the most constructivist category of teacher identified-the highly active computer-using teacher leader-is more than a full standard deviation more constructivist than the average teacher of the same subject, placing her roughly at the 87th percentile on that dimension. The difference is not as great for the "Group Work" component, nor when philosophy is controlled; however, even for those, the typical Computer-Using Teacher Leader is .75 standard deviations more constructivist than the average teacher of the same subject, putting her at the 77th percentile. The final area on which we compared Professionally Engaged Teachers according to the depth of their involvement in computer use was in terms of the objectives that they had for student computer use. Here, we omit the few Teacher Professionals and Teacher Leaders who did not have students use computers at all.

Among the remaining Professionally Engaged Teachers, though, there were substantial differences between the Highly Active Computer Users and the remaining Professionally Engaged Teachers in the objectives that they held for students when computers were in use. The objectives are shown in order from the ones chosen proportionally more often by less-active computer-using professionals to the objectives chosen proportionally more often by the Highly Active Computer-Using professionals (Teacher Leader and Teacher Professional categories combined for this analysis). The less active computer-users chose skills-oriented objectives (e.g., remediation and skills mastery) and collaboration objectives more than those Teacher Professionals who were Highly Active Computer Users. In contrast, Teacher Leaders and Professionals who fell into the high computer use category were more likely to select communications, presentation, and information gathering as their most important educational objectives for using technology. This suggests that even among and Teacher Leaders, depth of involvement with computers translates into a more constructivist exploitation of computer resources.

3

Teaching Computer Programmes

The CPU for this example is assumed to have a program counter (PC), an instruction register (IR), a single data register (R0), and a flags register (a few of whose constituent bits are shown individually). Instructions and data values each take up one "word"; addresses are the addresses of words (not of constituent bytes within words). The program, located in memory starting in word 0, calculates $\sum_{n=1}^{n=3} n$

memory location		*contents*	
0		LOAD	N
1		COMPARE	3
2		JUMP_IF_GREATER TO	9
3		ADD	SUM
4		STORE	SUM
5		LOAD	N
6		ADD	1
7		STORE	N
8		GOTO	0
9		STOP	
10	N	1	
11	SUM	0	

The program consists of a sequence of instructions occupying memory words 0-9; the data values are stored in the next two memory locations. The data locations are initialized before the program starts. The calculation is done with a loop. The loop starts by loading the current value of *N*. (Because the imaginary CPU only has one register, instructions like the "load" don't need to specify which register!) Once loaded, the value from variable *N* is checked to see whether it exceeds the required limit; the comparison instruction would set one of the "less than" (LT), "equal" (EQ), or "greater than" (GT) bits in the flags register.

The next instruction, the conditional jump in memory word 2, can cause a transfer to the STOP instruction following the loop and located in memory word 9. The jump will occur if the GT flag is set; otherwise the CPU would continue as normal with the next instructions in sequence. These instructions, in words 3 and 4, add the value of N into the accumulating total (held in SUM). The value of N is then incremented by 1 (instructions in words 5-7). Instruction 8 causes the CPU to reset the program counter so that it starts again at instruction 0. The first few steps are shown in Figure 1. Step 1 illustrates the fetch and decode steps for the first instruction, loading value from N (i.e. its initial value of 1). As each step is completed, the PC is incremented to hold the address of the next instruction. Steps 2, 3, and 4 illustrate the next few instruction cycles. If you could see inside a computer (or, at least, a simulator for a computer), this is the sort of process that you would observe.

Of course, if you could really see inside a computer as it ran, you wouldn't see "instructions" written out with names like COMPARE or LOAD, you wouldn't even see decimal numbers like 3 or 9. All that you would be able to

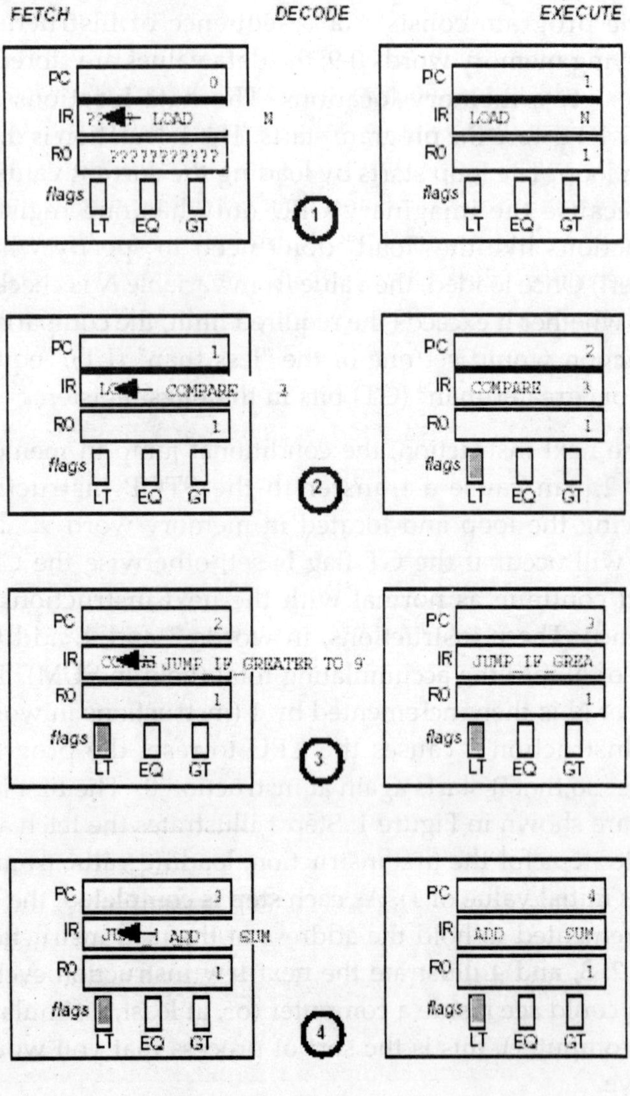

Figure. 1 Executing a program.

see would be "bitpatterns" --- the sequences of '1's and '0's in the words of memory or the registers of the CPU. So it would be something a little more like illustration Figure 2.

In order to be executed by a computer, a program must end up as a sequence of instructions represented by appropriate bit patterns in the memory of the computer. There is a very big gap between a statement of some problem that is to be solved by a computer program and the sequence of instruction bit patterns, and data bit patterns, that must be placed in the computer's memory so that they can be processed by the CPU.

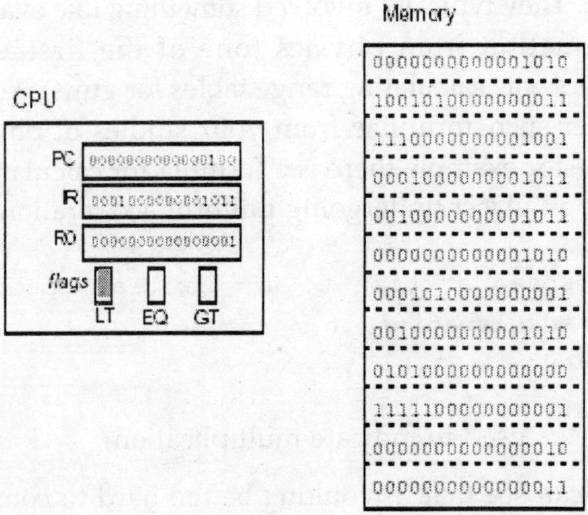

Figure 2 View into the machine.

You will be given a problem statement —

> "Get the computer to draw a tyrannosaurus rex chasing some corythosaurus plant eating dinosaurs." (Jurassic Park movie) "Program the computer to apply some rules to determine which bacterium caused this patient's meningitis." (Mycin diagnostic program) "Write a program that monitor's the Voice of America newswire and tells me about any news items that will interest me."

and you have to compose an instruction sequence. Hard work, but that is programming.

PROGRAMMING WITH BITS!

On the very first computers, in the late 1940s, programmers did end up deciding exactly what bit patterns would have to be placed in each word in the memory of their computer!

The programs that were being written were not that complex. They typically involved something like evaluating some equation from physics (one of the first uses of computers was calculating range tables for guns). You may remember such formulae from your studies of physics at school --- for example there is a formula for calculating the speed of an object undergoing uniform acceleration

```
v = speed at time t, u = initial speed,
a = acceleration, t = time
 v = u + a * t
```

(symbol * is used to indicate multiplication)

You can see that it wouldn't be too hard to compose a loop of instructions, like the loop illustrated at the start this chapter, that worked out v for a number of values of *t*. The programmer would write out the instruction sequence in rough on paper ...

```
...
load t
multiply a
add u
store v
...
```

Then it would be necessary to chose which memory word was going to hold each instruction and each data element, noting these address in a table:

```
start of loop @ location 108
end of loop @ location 120
variable t @ 156
```

Given this information it was possible to compose the bit patterns needed for each instruction. The early computers had relatively simple fixed layouts for their instruction words; the layout shown in Figure 3 would have been typical (though the number of operand bits would have varied).

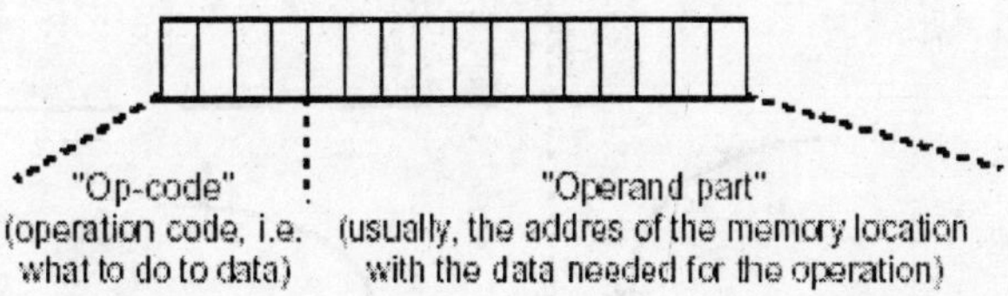

Figure 3 Simple layout for an instruction word

The programmer would have had a list of the bit patterns for each of the instructions that could be executed by the CPU

```
LOAD        0000      ADD         0001
STORE       0010      MULTIPLY    0011
SUBTRACT    0100      COMPARE     0101
...
```

The "op-code" part of an instruction could easily be filled in by reference to this table. Working out the "operand" part was a bit more difficult --- the programmer had to convert the word numbers from the address table into binary values.

Then, as shown in Figure 4, the complete instruction could be "assembled" by fitting together the bits for the opcode part and the bits for the address. The instruction still had to be placed into the memory of the machine. This would have been done using a set of switches on the front of the computer. One set of switches would have been set to represent the address for the instruction (switch down for a 0 bit, switch up for a 1). A second set of switches would have been set up with the bit pattern just worked out for that instruction. Then a "load address" button would have been pressed.

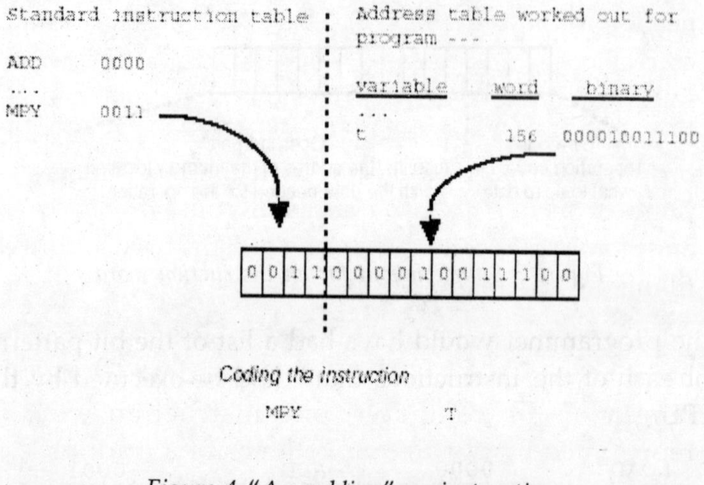

Figure 4 "Assembling" an instruction.

Every instruction in the program had to be worked out, and then loaded individually into memory, in this manner. As you can imagine, this approach to programming a computer was tedious and error prone. By 1949, bigger computers with more memory were becoming available. These had as many as one thousand words of memory (!) for storing data and programs. Toggling in the bit patterns for a program with several hundred instructions was simply not feasible. But the program preparation process started to become a little more sophisticated and a bit more automated. New kinds of programs were developed that helped the programmers in their task of composing programs to solve problems. These new software development aids were loaders and symbolic assemblers.

LOADERS

A "loader" is a fairly simple program. It reads in bit patterns representing the instructions (and initialized data elements) needed for a program, and stores these bit patterns in the correct locations in memory. The bit patterns were originally represented on media like punched cards or paper tapes (a hole in the card at particular position might represent a 1 bit, no hole meant a 0 bit). With the bit patterns were punched on cards, a loader program could read these cards and store the bit patterns, starting at some fixed address and filling out successive words.

The cards used typically had 12 rows where bits could be punched, and 80 columns. Depending on the word length of the computer, one instruction would be represented by two to four columns of a card; each card could hold the codes for twenty or more instructions. The "loader" program itself was typically about 10 instructions in length. It would get toggled into memory using the switches on the front of the computer (using the last few locations in memory, or some other area not used by the program being loaded).

The code of the loader would start by noting the address where the first instruction was to be placed. Then there would be a loop. In this loop, columns would be read from cards, instruction words built up from the bits read and, when complete would be stored in memory. As each instruction was stored, the loader would update its record of where to store the next. The loader would stop when it read some special end-marker bit pattern from a card. The person running the machine could then set the starting address for their program using the switches and set it running.

ASSEMBLERS

By 1950, programmers were using "assembler" programs to help create the bit pattern representation of the instructions. The difficult creative aspect of programming is deciding the correct sequence of instructions to solve the problem. Conversion of the chosen instructions to bit patterns is an essentially mechanical process, one that can be automated without too much difficulty. If an assembler was available, programmers could write out their programs using the mnemonic instruction names (LOAD, MULTIPLY, etc) and named data elements. Once the program had been drafted, it was punched on cards, one card for each instruction. This process produced the program source card deck, Figure 5. This "source" program was converted to binary instruction patterns by an assembler program (it "assembles" instructions). The source cards would be read by the assembler which would generate a binary card deck that could be loaded by the loader. The assembler program performs a translation process - converting the mnemonic instruction names and variable names into the correct bits. Assembler programs are meant to be fairly small (particularly the early ones that had to fit into a memory with only a few hundred words). Consequently, the translation task must not be complex.

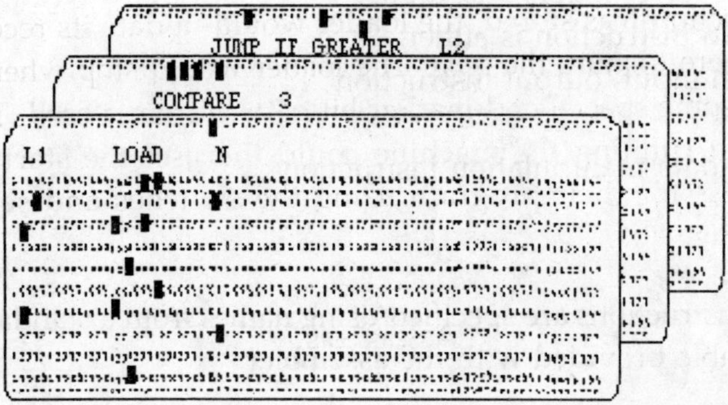

Figure 5 Assembly language source deck

"Assembly languages" are designed to have simple regular structures so that translation is easy. Assembly languages are defined by a few rules that specify the different kinds of instruction and data element allowed. In the early days, further rules specified how an instruction should be laid out on a card so as to make it even easier for the translation code to find the different parts of an instruction.

Syntax rules

Rules that specify the legal constructs in a language are that language's "syntax rules". For assembly languages, these rules are simple; for example, a particular assembly language might be defined by the following rules:

1. One statement per line (card).

2. A statement can be either:

An optional "label" at start and an instruction

or

a "label" (variable name) and a numeric value.

3. A "label" is a name that starts with a letter and has 6 or fewer letters and digits.
4. An instruction is either:
   an input/output instruction
   or
   a data manipulation instruction
   or
   ...

   Instructions are specified using names from a standard table provided with the assembler.

5. Labels start in column 1 of a card, instructions in column 8, operand details in column 15.

6. ...

An assembler program uses a table with the names of all the instructions that could be executed by the CPU. The instruction names are shortened to mnemonic abbreviations (with 3 letters or less) ...

```
LOAD                ---> L
ADD                 ---> A
STORE               ---> S
GOTO (JUMP)         ---> J
JUMP_IF_GREATER ---> JGT
MULTIPLY            ---> MPY
STOP (HALT)         ---> STP
COMPARE             ---> C
...
```

Short names of 1--3 characters require less storage space for this table (this was important in the early machines with their limited memories). If an assembly language is sufficiently restricted in this way, it becomes relatively simple to translate from source statements to binary code. The assembler program (translator) reads the text of an assembly language program twice, first working out information that it will need and then generating the bit patterns for the instructions. The first time the text is read, the assembler works out where to store each instruction and data element.

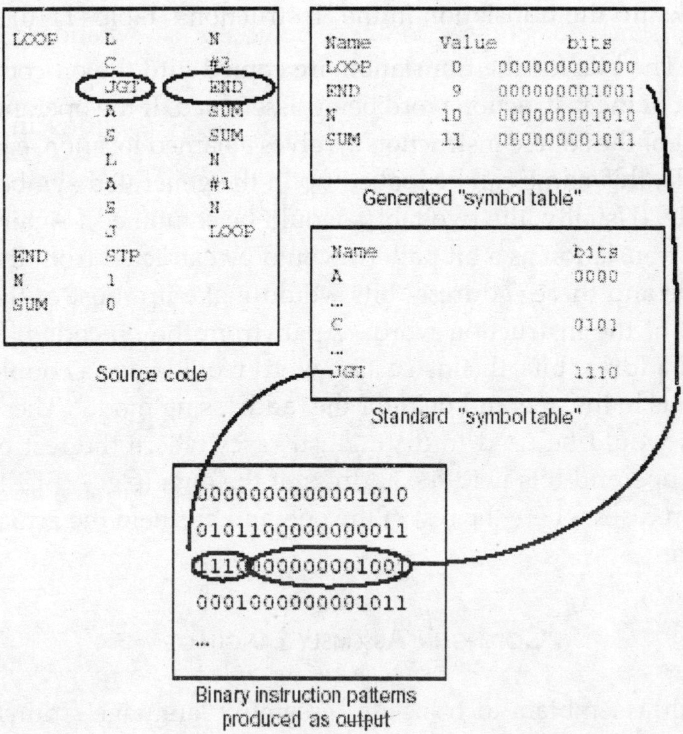

Figure. 6 Generating code in "pass 2" of the assembly process

This involves simply counting the cards (assembly language statements), and noting those where labels are defined. The names of the labels and the number of the card where they occurred are stored in a table that the assembler builds up in memory. The second time the source code is read, the assembler works out the bit patterns and saves them (by punching on cards - or in more modern systems by writing the information to a file). All the translation work is done in this second pass, see Figure 6. The translation is largely a matter of table lookup. The assembler program finds the characters that make up an instruction name, e.g. JGT, and looks up the translation in the "instructions" table (1110).

The bits for the translation are copied into the op-code part of the instruction word being assembled. If the operand part of the source instruction involves a named location, e.g. END, this name can be looked up in the generated symbol table. (Usually, the two tables would be combined.) Again, the translation as a bit pattern would be extracted from the table and these "address" bits would make up most of the rest of the instruction word. Apart from the op-code bits and address bits, the instruction word would have a couple of bits in the operand field for the "addressing mode". These bits would be used to distinguish cases where the rest of the operand bits held the address of the data (e.g. A SUM) from cases where the rest of the operand bits held the actual data.

Coding in Assembly Language

With assemblers to translate "assembly language" source code to bit patterns, and loaders to get the bits properly into memory, the programmers of the later '40s early '50s were able to forget about the bit patterns and focus more on problem solving and coding. Many of the details of coding were specific to a machine. After all, each different kind of CPU has a slightly different set of circuits for interpreting instructions and so offers a different set of instructions for the programmer to use. But there were basic coding patterns that appeared in slightly different forms in all programs on all machines. Programmers learnt these patterns—and used them as sort of building blocks that helped them work out an appropriate structure for a complete program.

Coding- sequence

The simplest pattern is the sequence of instructions:

```
L       TIME
MPY     ACCEL
A       U
S       V
```

This kind of code is needed at points in a program where some "formula" has to be evaluated.

Coding- choosing between alternative actions

Another very common requirement is to be able to chose between two (or more) alternatives. For example you might need to know the larger of two values that result from some other stage of some calculation:

```
if Velocity1 greater than Velocity2 then
maxvelocity equals Velocity1
otherwise maxvelocity equals Velocity2
```

Patterns for such "selection code" have to be organized around the CPU's instructions for testing values and making conditional jumps. A possible code pattern for selecting the larger of two values would be ...

```
load first value from memory into CPU register
compare with second value
jump if "less flag" is set to label L2
first value is the larger so just save it
store in place to hold larger
goto label L3
L2 load second value
store in place to hold larger
 L3 ... start instruction sequence that uses
 larger value
```

Similar code patterns would have existed for many other kinds of conditional test.

Coding- "subroutines"

"Sequence of statements", "selections using conditional tests", and "loops" are the basic patterns for organizing a particular calculation step. There is one other standard pattern that is very important for organizing a complete program - the subroutine. Typically, there will be several places in a program where essentially the same operation is needed. For example, a program might need to read values for several different data elements. Now the data values would be numbers that would have to end up being represented as integers in binary notation, but the actual input would be in the form of characters typed at a keyboard. It requires quite a lot of work to convert a character sequence, e.g. '1' '3' '4' (representing the number one hundred and thirty four), into the corresponding bit pattern (for 134 this is 0000000010000110).

The code involves a double loop --- one loop working through successive digits, inside it there would be a "wait loop" used to read a character from the keyboard. The code for number input would take at least 15 to 20 instructions. It wouldn't have been very practical to repeat the code at each point where a data value was needed. If the code were repeated everywhere it was needed, then all your memory would get filled up with the code to read your data and you wouldn't have any room for the rest of the program. Subroutines make it possible to have just one copy of some code, like the number input code (Figure 7 B).

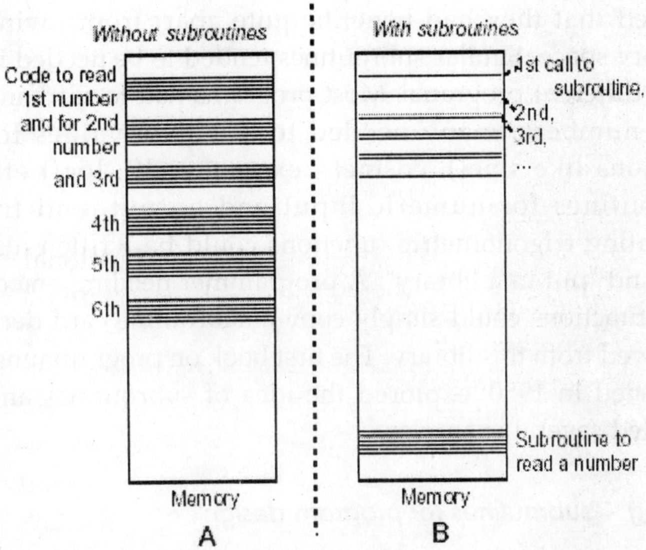

Figure 7. Sharing a piece of code as a subroutine.

At places where that code needs to be used, there is a "jump to subroutine" instruction. Executing this instruction causes a jump to the start of the code and, in some machine dependent way, keeps a record of where the main program should be resumed when the code is completed. At the end of the shared code, a "return from subroutine" instruction sets the program counter so as to resume the main program at the appropriate place.

Different computers have used quite distinct schemes for "saving the return address" --- but in all other respects they have all implemented essentially the same subroutine call and return scheme.

Coding- "subroutine libraries"

Subroutines first appeared about 1948 or 1949. It was soon realized that they had benefits quite apart from saving memory space. Similar subroutines tended to be needed in many different programs. Most programs had to read and print numbers; many needed to calculate values for functions like sine(), cosine(), exponential(), log() etc. Subroutines for numeric input and output, and for evaluating trigonometric functions could be written just once and "put in a library". A programmer needing one of these functions could simply copy a subroutine card deck borrowed from this library. The first book on programming, published in 1950, explored the idea of subroutines and included several examples.

Coding - "subroutines for program design"

It was also realized that subroutines provided a way of thinking about a programming problem and breaking it down into manageable chunks. Instead of a very long "main line program" with lots of loops and conditional tests, programs could have relatively simple main programs that were comprised mainly of calls to subroutines. Each subroutine would involve some sequential statements, loops, conditionals - and, possibly, calls to yet other subroutines. If a code segment is long and complex, with many nested loops and criscrossing jump (goto) instructions, then it becomes difficult to understand and the chances of coding errors are increased. Such difficulties could be reduced by breaking a problem down through the use of lots of subroutines each having a relatively simple structure.

Coding- data

Assembly languages do not provide much support for programmers when it comes to data. An assembly language will allow the programmer to attach a name to a word, or a group of memory words. The programmer has to chose how many memory words will be needed to represent a data value (one for an integer, two/ four or more for a real number, or with text some arbitrary number of words depending on the number of characters in the text "string".) The programmer can not usually indicate that a memory word (or group of words) is to store integer data or real data, and certainly the assembler program won't check how the data values are used. In the early days of programming, programmer's distinguished two kinds of data:

Globals

> The programmers would arrange a block of memory to hold those variables that represented the main data used by the program and which could be accessed by the main program or any of the subroutines.

Locals

> Along with the code for each subroutine, the programmer would have allocated any variables needed to hold temporary results etc. These were only supposed to be used in that subroutine and so were "local" to the routine.

The organization of memory in an early computer is shown in Figure 8. The "local" data space for each subroutine was often located immediately after the code, so mixing together code and data parts of a program. Many machines were designed around the concept of "global" and "local" data. These machine architectures reserved specific memory addresses for global data and provided special "addressing modes" for accessing global and local data elements. Different memory organizations were proposed in the early 1960s in association with the development of the "Algol" languages.

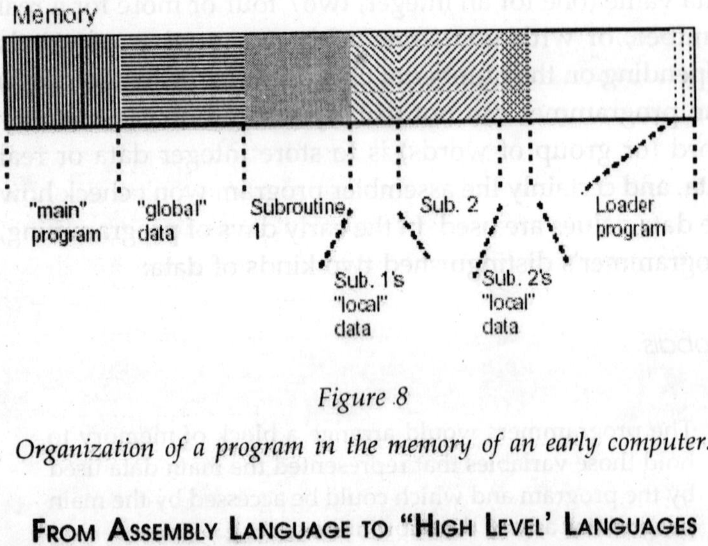

Figure 8

Organization of a program in the memory of an early computer.

From Assembly Language to "High Level' Languages

In the 1950s, most programs were written in assembly language. But assembly languages have disadvantages - they involve the programmer in too much detail. The programmer is stuck with thinking about "instructions in the computer". Now sometimes one does want to chose the instruction sequence; people still program in assembly language when dealing with small sections of time critical code. But for most programming tasks, one doesn't really want to get down to the level of detail of choosing individual instructions. Starting in the mid-50s, "higher level programming languages" began to appear. Initially they did little more than provided packaged versions of those coding patterns that assembly language programmers were already familiar with. Thus a "high level programming language" might provide some kind of "DO- loop" ...

```
DO 10 IT = 1, 4
...
10 CONTINUE
```

Here, the programmer has specified that a sequence of statements (...) is to be executed 4 times. It is fairly easy to translate such a high level specification of a loop into assembly language code with all the instructions for comparisons, conditional tests, jumps etc. When programming in a high level language, the programmer no longer has to bother about individual instructions. Instead, the programmer works at a higher level of abstraction - more remote from machine details. Automatic translation systems expand the high level code into the instruction sequences that must be placed in the computer's memory.

Over time, high level languages have evolved to take on more responsibilities and to do more for the programmer. But in most high level languages, you can still see the basic patterns of "instruction sequence", "loop", "conditional tests for selection", and "subroutines" that have been inherited from earlier assembly language style programming.

Back in the early 1950s there were very few computers. Large universities might have one, as might government research laboratories, and a few big companies. A scientist of engineer wanting to run a program would book time on the machine. When their turn came, they would be totally in control of "THE COMPUTER". They had to load the assembler (or high level language translator), use it to convert their program to binary instruction format, load the binary version of their program, start their program using the switches on the front of the computer, feed data cards to their program as it ran, etc. It all involved a lot of running around fiddling with card readers (and, later on, magnetic tapes), pressing buttons, flicking switches. Most people didn't do the job very well and wasted a lot of the time that they had booked on the machine.

Organizations that had computers soon started to employ professional "computer operators". Computer operators were responsible for getting maximum use out of the computing equipment. They would run the language translators and assemblers for users, they would load binary card decks and get the programs run. Since they worked full time with the computers, they were familiar with the all the operating procedures involved and so made many fewer mistakes and wasted much less time. Since users no longer directly controlled the running of their programs, they had to write "job control instructions" for the operators. These job control instructions would tell the operators of any special requirements such as the need to mount a particular magnetic tape on which a program was to store some generated data.

Computers were changing rapidly in the early '50s. Peripheral devices were becoming more complex and versatile. Many could operate semi-autonomously. They could accept a direction from the CPU telling them to transfer some data and could organize the data transfers so that these occurred while the CPU continued executing a program. Such changes made for more efficient program execution because the CPU spent less time waiting for data transfers. But such changes also meant that the code to control peripheral devices became a lot more complex. Any erroneous I/O code could seriously disrupt the workings of the computer system and might even result in damage to peripheral devices or to media like magnetic tapes or punched cards. Originally, a programmer would have been able to use all of the computer's memory (if possible, the area with the loader program was left alone so that the loader code wouldn't have to be toggled into memory again).

The requirements of the new peripheral devices made it advantageous to reserve a part of memory for "systems code" - the specialized code that controlled the new devices. The new organization for main memory is shown in Figure 9; part of memory is reserved for the "system's code" (and, also, for system's data - the system needed memory space to record information such as identifiers associated with magnetic tapes on different tape decks). The "systems" area of memory had subroutines for whole variety of input output tasks. There would have been a subroutines to handle tasks such as reading one character from the control keyboard or one column of a punched card. Another routine would exist to organize the transfer of the contents of a number of words of memory (containing binary data) to a tape block.

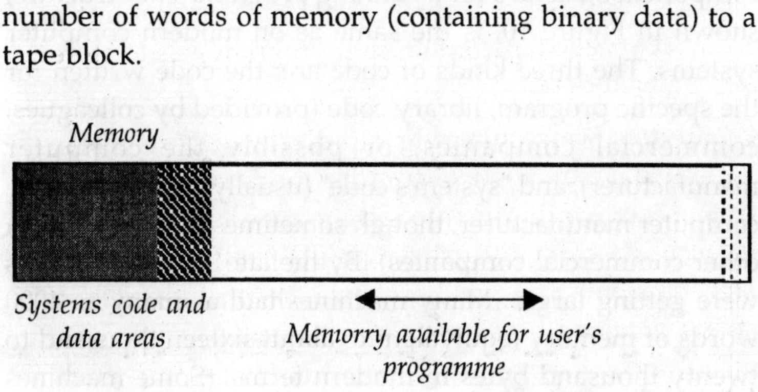

Figure. 9 Part of main memory is reserved for "system's" code and data.

Programmers could have calls to these "systems subroutines" in the code of their programs. (Later, if you study computer architecture and operating systems you will learn why a specialized variant on the JSR subroutine call instruction was added to the CPU's instruction set. This specialized instruction would have had a distinct name, e.g. "trap" or "supervisor call (svc)". Calls to the systems subroutines were made using this "system call" instruction rather than the normal JSR jump to subroutine.) Usually, rather than making direct calls to the "system's code" programmers continued to make use of library routines. For example, a program might use a number input routine. This routine would read characters punched on a card (making a call to one of the systems' input routines to get each character in turn) and would convert the character sequence to a numeric value represented as a bit pattern. There would be two such input routines (one for integers, the other for real numbers). There would be corresponding output routines that could generate character sequences that could be printed on a line printer.

These early systems established a kind of three component structure for a running program. The structure, shown in Figure 10, is the same as on modern computer systems. The three kinds of code are: the code written for the specific program, library code (provided by colleagues, commercial companies, or possibly the computer manufacturer), and "system's code" (usually provided by the computer manufacturer, though sometimes purchased from other commercial companies). By the late 1950s, memories were getting larger. Many machines had as many as 4000 words of memory (equivalent to about sixteen thousand to twenty thousand bytes in modern terms). Some machines had as much as 32000 words of memory. These larger

Figure 10

System's code, library code, and user's code.

memories allowed the systems code to be extended in other ways that could improve the utilization and performance of the computer system.

Quite substantial amounts of time tended to be wasted between jobs and between each phase of a job. For example a user might submit a job written in the high level language Fortran along with a deck of data cards to be processed. The operator would have to load the Fortran compiler (translator) and feed in the cards with the program; the translator would output assembly language code that would be punched on cards or written to tape. When the compiler stopped, the operator had to load the assembler program and feed in the generated assembly language source, along with source card decks for any assembly language library routines the user had requested. The assembler would produce binary code (on cards or tape).

The operator then had to load the binary and start the program running. Once the program was running, the operator had to feed in the data cards. When the program stopped, the operator had to collect up cards and printed output and then reset the machine ready for the next job. Each of these steps would involve the operator attending card readers, punches, tape decks, and control consoles. If a computer system only had card input and output, the entire process was very slow. It could take several minutes to load a Fortran translator, run a user program through the translator and punch a deck of cards with the assembly language translation.

Most large systems would have had several tape decks which made things a little easier. But it was still an involved process; the operator would have to work at the control switches on the front of the computer, entering instructions that would cause the computer to load the translator or assembler program from tape, then setting the switches again before starting the loaded program. The process is illustrated in the various panes in Figure 11.

The computer system would have had four or more tape decks; one would have the tape with the code for the compiler, the other would have the assembler. The other two tape decks would hold work tapes where intermediate results could be written. The operator would start by loading the compiler into memory and putting the card deck with program and data on the card reader. When the compiler had been loaded, the operator would use the control switches to start it running. The compiler would read the cards with the source code and generate assembly language that would be written to tape. The operator then had to rewind this tape, and load the assembler. The assembler then had to be run; it would read its input from the first work tape and produce the binary code (with the bit patterns for instructions) on a second work tape. When the assembler finished, the operator again had to rewind a tape and then again get a program (now the user's program) loaded into memory. Finally, the user's program could be started. It would read its data cards and produce output on a line printer.

Every time the operator had to do something like enter data on switches or rewind a tape, the CPU would be left idle. Since operators wouldn't know how long it would take to translate a program, or assemble it, or run it, they couldn't be instantly ready to start the next step in the process. So time was inevitably wasted. The CPUs were desperately expensive (CPUs with a fraction of the power of a modern personal computer would have costed millions of dollars) so it was very important to try to keep them working as much as possible.

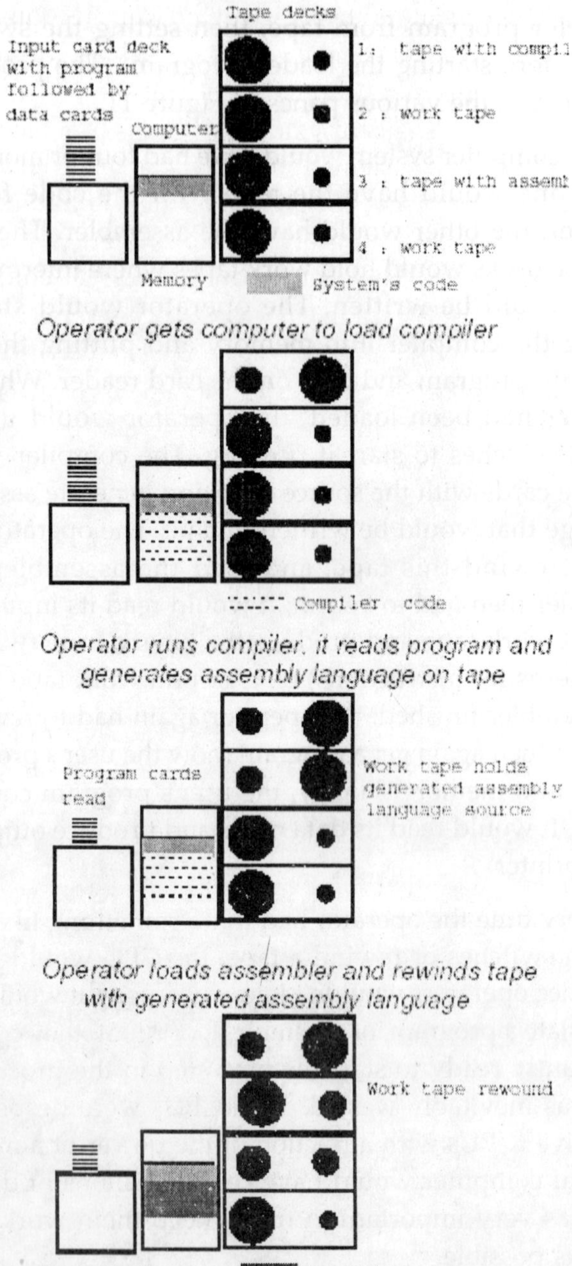

Figure. 11 Operating the computer.

Most of the operators' tasks involved simple, routine things that could be automated and speeded up. Control routines were written to automate the routine tasks like loading the compiler and rewinding a tape. This control code was added to the systems' i/o code in the reserved area of memory. These control programs, written to automate routine tasks for the computer operators, were the first "Operating Systems". They worked by reading "control cards" and performing standard actions. Programs were submitted along with "job control cards" that could be interpreted by the computer's control program. An input card deck (circa ~1960) would have been something like the following:

```
JOB         USERNAME
FORTRAN     ...
C MY PROGRAM TO COMPUTE HEAT FLOW
  IN REACTOR DIMENSION A(10,10)
  ...
  END
ASSEMBLE        ...
LINK            ...
RUN
       1.2      4.5
ENDJOB
```

The control program used the control cards like the "JOB" card. These would have a keyword (and usually additional information, the JOB card might have identified the user who was to be charged). A job would be terminated by an ENDJOB card; if anything went wrong (like a coding error detected by the compiler or an arithmetic error during execution) the operating system could tidy up by reading all remaining cards in the card reader until it found the ENDJOB. The operating system code handled each control card in a standard way. When it read a JOB card, it would print an accounting message on the operator's terminal.

A FORTRAN card was processed by loading the FORTRAN compiler into memory and then "calling" it to read all the FORTRAN source cards. The operating system would also arrange for an output tape to be ready for the compiler to use. If there were no compile errors, the operating system organized the rewinding of the output tape and the loading of the assembler. The other steps, like the linking process where "library" code was read from tapes were handled in similar fashion. If the process resulted in successful construction of an executable program, this was then "RUN" so that it could process its data cards. The FORTRAN compiler, the ASSEMBLER, the LINKER, and the user program were all executed rather as if they were subroutines called by the controlling operating system.

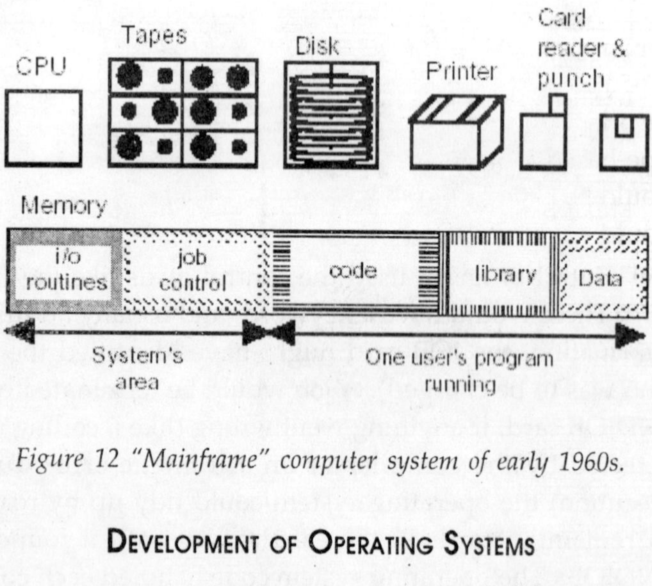

Figure 12 "Mainframe" computer system of early 1960s.

DEVELOPMENT OF OPERATING SYSTEMS

By the early 1960s, the larger computer systems had the

form shown in Figure 12. Disks were not common, most systems made do with tape decks. An early disk unit would have been about five feet high, would have had a multi-platter arrangement with disks about 18 inches across. A complete disk unit would have held about as much data as a modern floppy and would have costed - well certainly more than a new car, probably something close to the price of a small suburban house. Most of the computers of the time got by with just tapes, but some had disks. Disks were a lot faster than tapes (faster transferring data, no need to read all the data sequentially because the disk control could move the disk heads to the blocks containing the specific data required, no need to "rewind", ...).

A disk unit could substitute for several tapes. Space on the disk would be partitioned: e.g. blocks 0-159 holding the FORTRAN compiler, 160-235 holding the COBOL compiler, 236-263 with the RPG compiler, 264-274 for the ASSEMBLER, 275-304 containing the FORTRAN subroutine library, 305-310 for the LINKER, 311- 410 for "workspace 1", 411-511 for "workspace 2". But even if a disk was being used, the operations remained much the same as described for the tape-based machines. Part of the machine's main memory would be reserved for the primitive Operating System. This would have consisted of a set of standard i/o subroutines that controlled the various peripheral devices and the subroutines that interpreted the job control cards. In addition to this Operating System (OS), the computer would have a number of pieces of software supplied by its manufacturer:

- — FORTRAN compiler (translator for a programming language intended for use by scientists and engineers)
- — FORTRAN subroutine libraries (by now these would contain subroutines for doing things like sorting,

complex mathematical operations like 'matrix inversion', as well as more standard things like converting digits to numeric values or calculating SINE(), LOG() etc)

— COBOL compiler (translator for a business programming language) and others.

The job control component of the OS minimized the time needed by the operators to set up the machine between successive jobs, and the time spent organising successive phases of an individual job. The system's i/o routines could arrange for i/o to proceed simultaneously with computations. Together these improved the efficiency of machine usage. But there were problems. For example:

— CPU usage was still relatively low. Even with smart peripherals running simultaneously with computations, most programs spent a large amount of time (often 50% or more) in "wait loops" waiting for input data to be read from devices, or waiting for output data to be printed.

— Programmers were inconvenienced by slow turn around and lack of opportunity to test and debug their programs. (It was common to have to wait 24 hours for results to be returned, and the 'results' might be simply a statement to the effect that the compiler had found the second card of the program to be wrongly punched!)

— Some programs needed more memory than could be obtained.

These problems, and other related problems, were dealt with in a series of developments undertaken throughout the

1960s and early 1970s that lead to more sophisticated operating systems.

Multiprogramming

The most pressing problem was the "waste" of CPU cycles when the single job in the computer's memory had to wait for an i/o transfer to complete. The CPU was by far the most costly part of the computer system of this period. The prices of other components like the peripherals and memory were falling. Larger memories were practical. The availability of larger main memories provided the solution to the problem of keeping the CPU busy. If a single job in main memory couldn't keep the CPU occupied all the time, then have two or more jobs in memory (Figure 13).

The computer's memory was be split up into "partitions".

— One held the OS.

— Another (tiny) part would hold the 'boot' loader (the name 'boot' loader apparently relates to some argument that starting the computer using this loader to read the OS from tape/disk was like 'picking oneself up by one's bootstraps'. ?. !)

— The rest of memory was split up among two, three or more program partitions.

A user's program would be run in a partition in much the same way as it had previously been run using all memory not allocated to the OS. In the early versions of this scheme, only the CPU and the OS were shared. Each memory "partition" had to have its own assigned peripheral devices - a line printer, a card reader, two or more tape decks, and a separate allocation of space on disk (if there was a disk).

The OS had to be more elaborate because it had to keep track of each of the different jobs and of the way peripheral devices had been allocated to jobs. If a job asked the OS to perform some i/o operation that involved delays, the OS had to switch the CPU to execute instructions for a job in a different memory partition. Really, the more elaborate OS was using a computer with a large memory to simulate the working of two (or more) smaller, slower computers! The "partitioning" of memory was adjustable.

The operators could enter commands at the control terminal that would get the OS to rearrange the way memory was used. For example, in the morning the operators might arrange to have two medium sized partitions to run average jobs. In the afternoon, when lots of programmers had submitted programs that needed small test runs, the operators could reconfigure the machine to have three small partitions. Overnight, the machine would be used with all the non-OS memory in a single partition so as to allow bigger programs to run. The human operators were involved in the relatively slow, and infrequent, process of reconfiguring the machine for a different degree of "multiprogramming".

The process of switching the CPU among the different programs was all done automatically, in mere millisecond times, under the control of the of code in the OS. Switching would normally happen only when a running job made a request for i/o to the OS; a request like "card reader, read a card and store all 80 characters in this portion of memory ...", or "line printer, this portion of memory holds the 132 characters to be printed on a line, please print them", or "tape drive 8, transfer your next data block into memory starting here ...". The OS would get the device to start the data transfer, and arrange to be notified when the transfer

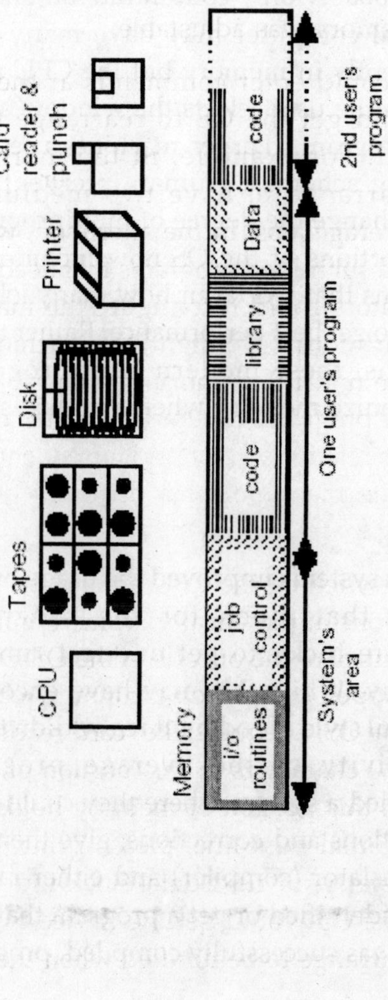

Figure 13

Early multiprogrammed system.

was complete. But the requesting program usually wouldn't be able to continue until the transfer was done - so the OS switched the CPU to work for another program.

Essentially all operating systems now use some form of multiprogramming system. Support for multiprogramming may be limited in an OS for a personal computer (after all a personal computer is to be used by just one person and that person can probably only concentrate on one thing at a time); a personal computer may have many different programs concurrently in memory but the CPU may only get switched when the user selects the window associated with a different program. Larger machines use elaborate multiprogramming schemes. Human intervention is no longer needed to change the degree of multiprogramming. The job control portions of the OS now include code for elaborate algorithms that work out how many jobs should be allowed to run to get best performance. Rather than fixed memory partitions, these modern multiprogramming systems can reorganize memory whenever this is found to be necessary.

Timesharing

Multiprogrammed systems improved the usage of the CPU - but didn't do that much for the programmers. Programmers were lucky to get one test run of their programs each day. While this may have encouraged a meticulously careful style of coding it really didn't do much for the productivity of the average programmer. Programmers needed a system where they could edit their code making additions and corrections, give the new code to a language translator (compiler) and either rapidly get any coding errors identified or get a program that could be run. If a program was successfully compiled, programmers needed to make small test runs that allowed their programs to be tested with small data sets.

"Timesharing" systems, pioneered at MIT in Boston USA starting around 1960, provided programmers with more appropriate development environments. It was the development of disk (and drum) storage that made these new systems possible. (Drums have ceased to be used. They are a variation on disks in which data is recorded in tracks on a cylinder rather than on a flat platter. Each track had its own read-write head, see Figure 14. Drums were a lot faster than disks, but the multiple read-write heads made them expensive. They have gone out of fashion because their maximum storage capacity is a lot less than a disk.) The CPU of MIT's original time-sharing computer was a slightly modified version of the largest computer then commercially available - an IBM 7094. The machine had two blocks of memory, both with 32K (i.e. 32768) words. One block of memory held the operating system. The other held the program and data for a single user. The computer had several very large disks with a total capacity of several million words of storage (~50 Megabyte in modern terms?).

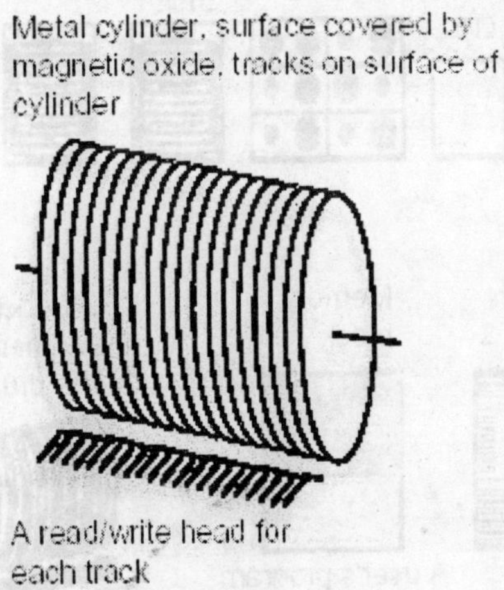

Figure 14 Drum storage.

The computer was intended to support up to 32 people working simultaneously. Users worked at 'teletypes' (a kind of electric typewriter) that were connected to the computer via a special controller (see Figure 15). Only one user's program was actually running at any time. It was the program that was currently in memory. The other 'users' would be waiting. Their programs would be saved on the drum. A user's program was allowed to run until either it asked the OS to arrange some input or output (to the user's teletype or to a disk file); or until a 'time quantum' expired. (A time quantum might be ~ 0.1 seconds.) When a program asked for i/o or used up its time quantum it would be 'swapped out to the drum'. 'Swapping out' meant that the content of user memory was written to the drum. A different user's program would then be 'swapped in'. This program would then be allowed to run until it exceed its time quantum or asked for i/o. The second program would then get swapped out and a third program would be swapped in.

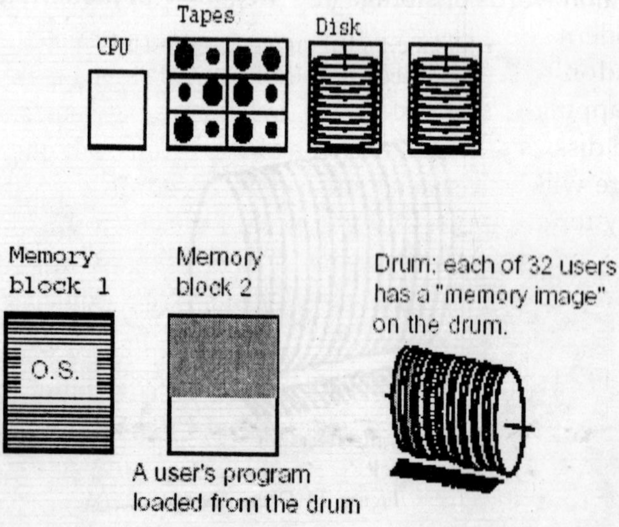

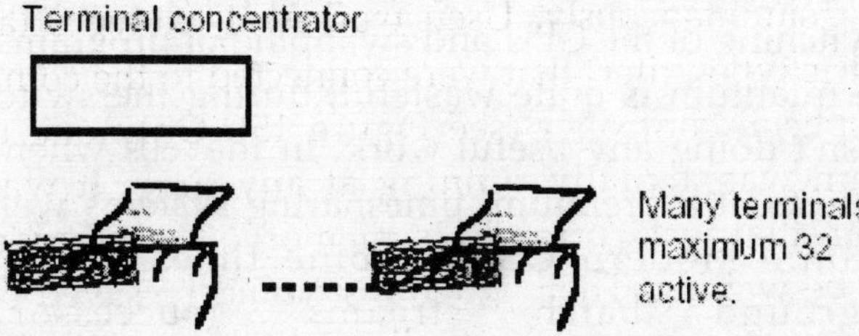

Figure 15 MIT's pioneering "time-sharing" computer system.

Eventually, it would be program one's turn to run again. Even if the system was very busy with lots of users, each individual user would get ~0.1 seconds worth of CPU time every three seconds. So it would seem to an individual user that their program was running continuously, albeit on a rather slow computer. Operating systems for personal computers don't use timesharing. (They are personal computers because you don't want to share!) But most other operating systems (e.g. the Unix system you may use in more advanced CS subjects) incorporate sophisticated versions of the timesharing scheme pioneered by MIT. Modern computer systems have much more memory and so don't have to do quite as much "swapping"; but swapping is still necessary. (Swaps are between memory and disk as the machines won't have drums; but quite often there will be a special small high speed disk that is used only for swapping and not to hold files.) If you get to use Unix, you will notice when you've been "swapped out"! (The machine seems to ignore you.)

There are obvious similarities in "multiprogramming" and "timesharing"; both involve the OS controlling the use of a computer system so that it appears as several computers (lots of little ones, or lots of slow ones). Multiprogramming and timesharing evolved to meet different needs;

multiprogramming was to optimize CPU usage, timesharing was an attempt to optimize programmer usage! The switching of the CPU and swapping of programs after a time quantum is quite wasteful; during the switch the CPU isn't doing any useful work. In the '60s when CPU power was at a premium, timesharing systems were not common. Modern OSs combine timesharing with "background batch streams" (successor to multiprogramming) to get the best of both approaches. If no interactive user needs the CPU, the OS allocates it to a long running, multi-programmed "background job".

File Management

Users of the MIT system were able to keep their own files on disk. Operating systems had to be extended quite a lot before they could allow users to have their own files like this. The first disks were limited in capacity and all their storage capacity was needed for systems software - compilers, assemblers, subroutine libraries, work areas for the compilers etc. As suggested in an earlier example, the system's administrator could allocate the space; e.g. "FORTRAN compiler in blocks 0..159" etc. This was adequate when there wasn't much disk space and whatever there was had all to be used for systems software.

As disks got larger, it became possible to allow users to have some space. But this space couldn't be allocated to users in the same way as the system's administrator had allocated it for systems software. It was no good telling a user "You can have blocks 751 to 760" because they'd make mistakes and use blocks 151 to 160 (and so overwrite the compiler!). Every attempt by a user program to read from or to write to the disk has to be checked another task for the OS. The OS has to keep records of the disk space used by each user.

The simple form of "file directory" has to be made more elaborate to suit a shared environment. In shared environments, the disk directories contain details of file ownership and access permissions as well as the standard information like file name and block allocation. The time-shared computer systems started to have files owned by the operating system with lists of the names of users; the main directory on the disk would have an individual directory for each user. These individual directories contained details of the files belonging to that user. The OS could impose restrictions on the number of files, or total space allocated to an individual user. Users could specify that they wanted files to be private, or to be readable by other users in a cooperative work group. Once the OS had acquired records of users, it could keep records of jobs run, CPU time consumed and so forth. Previously, such accounting information had had to be manually logged by the computer operators. By the mid to late 1960s, these accounting tasks had become another responsibility of the OS; the operators merely had to run a program that printed out the bills that had been calculated using the information that the OS had stored.

Virtual Memory

In the late '50s and early '60s, computer memories were still quite small; it was rare for a computer to have more than 32K (32768) words of main memory (in modern terms, that is about 120,000 to 160,000 bytes). Some of this memory had to be reserved for the OS. This meant that programmers were limited in the amount of code and data that they could get in memory. Once disks became available, schemes were devised that allowed programmers to have programs and data that exceeded the machine's main memory capacity. When the programming was running, only parts of its code and data would be in main memory, the rest would be on disk. Initially, individual programmers were responsible for organizing their program code and data so that both could be stored partly in memory and partly on disk. As shown in Figure 16, the programmer had to break up a program into groups of subroutines that got used in the same "phases" of a program. A program would typically start by using one group of routines (some taken from a library) to read in data, then another group of routines would do calculations needed to set up for the main processing phase, a different group of routines would do the main calculations, another calculation phase would follow to get results that were to be printed, and then some routines would be used in an output phase. At any one time, only a few of the routines needed to be in main memory.

The program would have some fixed amount of space for code in main memory. The complete program was stored on disk (spread over many disk blocks). When the program was run, a small part of this code would have to be in main memory. This chunk of code would have included the main program, and any frequently used subroutines. The main program had to have extra code to load the different 'overlays' as each was needed. It would start by loading the 'overlay' with the input routines (Figure 16A). Once the main program had loaded the input 'overlay' it would call the input routines; these would read the program's data. When the input phase was complete, the main program would resume and arrange the loading of code for phase 1 of the calculations. The phase 1 routines would then be called (Figure 16B). The main program would continue by loading the overlay with the routines for the next phase. The phase 2 routines would then be executed (Figure 16C). The program would continue in this way, loading each bit of code as it was needed.

As well as bothering about shuffling the code between disk and main memory, the programmers had to devise equally complex schemes to shuffle their data. It was very common to have far more data than would fit in main memory. For example, an engineer who wanted to model heat flow in a metal beam might need to work out the temperature at successive time intervals at a number of points on the beam. To get meaningful results, the engineer would have needed a fairly fine grid of points, e.g. modelling 1000 points along the beam and 100 points across the beam. But you can't fit 100,000 real numbers into main memory if you've only got 32K words for the OS, your program and your data.

When shuffling code, programmers had standard 'overlay' models to follow. When shuffling data, they were on their own and had to invent their own schemes (because the best way of shuffling data between memory and disk depends on the frequency of access and the access patterns used in a particular program). This need to bother about shuffling code and data around was a distraction. It didn't have anything to do with solving a problem (like working out something about heat flow in beams); it was simply a matter of fighting with limitations of the computing systems available. The programmers just wanted big programs with big "address spaces", but they were being forced to think in terms of a two level storage system - the main memory, and a secondary disk memory.

Another extension to the computer's operating system hid the sordid details of the "two level store" from the programmers. With a little help from some special extra hardware in the CPU, an OS can be made to fake things, so that it seems as if a computer has a very much larger memory than it really does possess. The OS can arrange to know which parts of a program's code and data are in memory and which parts are on disk. When a chunk of code or data not in memory is needed, the OS can shuffle things around to get that code or data into memory.

The programmer need never know that this is happening. The Atlas computer built by the University of Manchester, England, around about 1960 was the first with what was then called a "one level store". It combined 16K words of real memory and storage on a drum. The OS, and special "paging" hardware in the CPU, faked things so that the Atlas machine seemed to be a computer with one million words of memory. It took more than ten years before these memory management schemes became widely used on large computers. The name for the scheme was changed to virtual storage or virtual memory. (The use of the word virtual is slightly odd. It is really the same usage as in optics where one talks of "virtual images" being produced by magnifying glasses and by mirrors.

The virtual store isn't real store - it just looks that way. The term has acquired wider usage, so multiprogramming is now sometimes discussed in terms of virtual processors - the OS makes it look as if you have many processors. "Virtual reality" is the latest extension.) In addition to special "paging" hardware that is needed in the CPU, support for virtual memory requires a lot more code in the OS. But now it is all commonplace; the CPU chips and OSs even for personal computers started to support virtual memory in the late 1980s.

Spooling

Developers of Operating Systems found yet another way in which they could make the OS fake things so that the computer seemed different from what it really was. A program that wants to print data can ask the OS - "please send this information to the line printer". But what happens if you have a multiprogrammed computer, where the execution of several programs is being interleaved, and more than one of the programs wants to print data? It obviously won't do to have a program print a line or two then stop, have another program start and print a line, then the first program resume. Interleaved printouts aren't much use. The first solution was a little expensive; you had to have many peripheral devices. If you intended to have 4 memory partitions, for 4-way multiprogramming, then you had had to buy four separate printers. Although printer manufacturers liked this scheme, it was not widely popular. Eventually, once most systems were equipped with disks, the OS developers found a work around. Programmers never send output directly to devices like printers - they merely think they do.

The OS fakes it so that each program that wants to print thinks that it has its own exclusive printer ("virtual printers"). Rather than send output directly to a device like a printer, the OS would collect ("spool up") all the output from the program and save it in a temporarily allocated file on disk. Each running program could be allocated a separate area on disk to store its output temporarily. When a program finished, the file containing the output that it had written was tidied up by the OS and then transferred to a queue. A little printer control program would form another part of the OS. It would run the printer(s) attached to the computer. For each printer that the system had, the print control program would take a file from the output queue and arrange to get it printed in one piece. As each print file finished, the print control program would arrange to take the next file from the head of the output queue.

Late 1960s early 1970s system

By the late 1960s early 1970s, Operating Systems were becoming large and complex. The figure shows some of the software components that would have made up the OS in memory (the relative sizes of components are not significant).

There would be a number of i/o handling routines. These would include "device driver" routines that organize data transfers to/from peripheral devices. Other routines would deal with 'interrupts' that devices use to indicate when they've completed a data transfer. The OS would respond to interrupts by updating its records of which programs were waiting for i/o. Another large chunk of code would be devoted to "process management", i.e. the scheduling of the allocation of the CPU, the processor, to programs. This code kept track of which programs were ready to use the CPU and which were waiting for i/o from terminals, or disks, or other devices. If the system supported interactive users with 'time sharing', this scheduling code had to make sure that no program ran for too long without stopping to let other programs have some CPU cycles.

There would be complex rules to apply to determine which to pick if there were several multiprogrammed jobs ready to run. The system would typically have a large number of jobs queued up on disk, these queued jobs would have been read earlier from cards. Another part of "process management" code would be run regularly to check whether any queued job should be started. The system would have some routines for interpreting the cards with "Job Control Language" (JCL) statements that specify the various processing steps a job required. "JOB" cards would have information that the JCL interpreter had to check to identify the job's owner (so that accounts could be kept and file use could be checked). Other JCL cards would specify things like the compiler (translator) to be used, or files needed to hold data.

File management

File management code would take up another large chunk of memory. This code would allow users to create files to store programs or data on disk; checks would have to be made to restrict users to allowed disk quotas, other checks would be made to see that only authorized users could access a file, and the code would have to make certain that disk blocks were allocated properly so that files didn't get mixed up.

File management code also had to look after things like providing temporary files for 'spooling' program output, special files for "swapping" timeshared programs, and other special files that modelled "virtual memory" for big programs. Memory management code would organize the allocation of main memory to user's programs. This might be something relatively easy, like maintaining a fixed number of 'partitions' in which programs could run. Where used, things like "virtual memory" made memory management a lot more complex. There would be some code used to keep accounts so that people could be charged for their computer usage. The OS code would also include minor specialized components like the "spooler". All of the code components in the OS would have needed their own tables of data, these data tables would have taken up another area of memory.

Networking

Originally, computers were located in isolated, air-

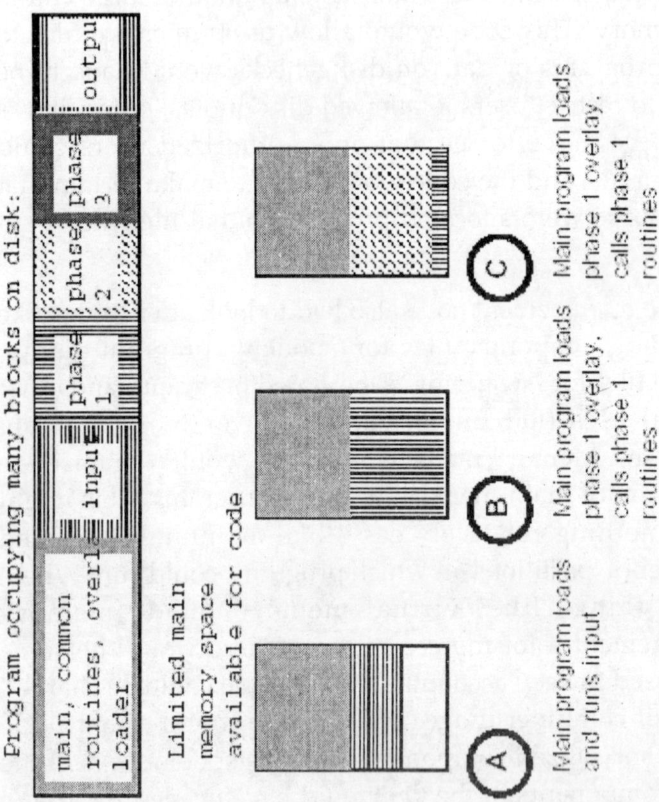

Figure 16 Program "overlay" scheme.

conditioned computer rooms and they communicated only through their card readers, line printers, and the operators control terminal. Gradually, they began to be linked up. It was limited at first:

— machines like the MIT time-share machine would be connected to many terminals in surrounding buildings,

— a university with a central computer might have extra line printers and card readers located off campus at research centres; these would be linked to the computer by specially installed non-standard telephone lines.

The first real networked systems would have been the US's SAGE air defence system and the air-line seat reservation systems. These were fairly specialized.

The main computer only ran a single program. SAGE had a program that kept track of aircraft movements; the seat reservation systems looked after files that contained details of bookings for each scheduled flight in the next couple of weeks. The main computers were linked by special high-speed "leased line" telephone connections to smaller computers in other towns. These smaller computers acted as concentrators for messages coming from many terminals, either directly connected terminals or terminals linked via slow-speed telephone connections, see Figure 17.

During the 1960s, a number of organizations like large banks and airlines started to "network" their computer systems. But the scope was always fairly limited. The organizations had a main computer that ran one program - a seat reservation program, or a bank accounting record keeping program ("transaction programs" they keep track of individual transaction like the cashing of a check).

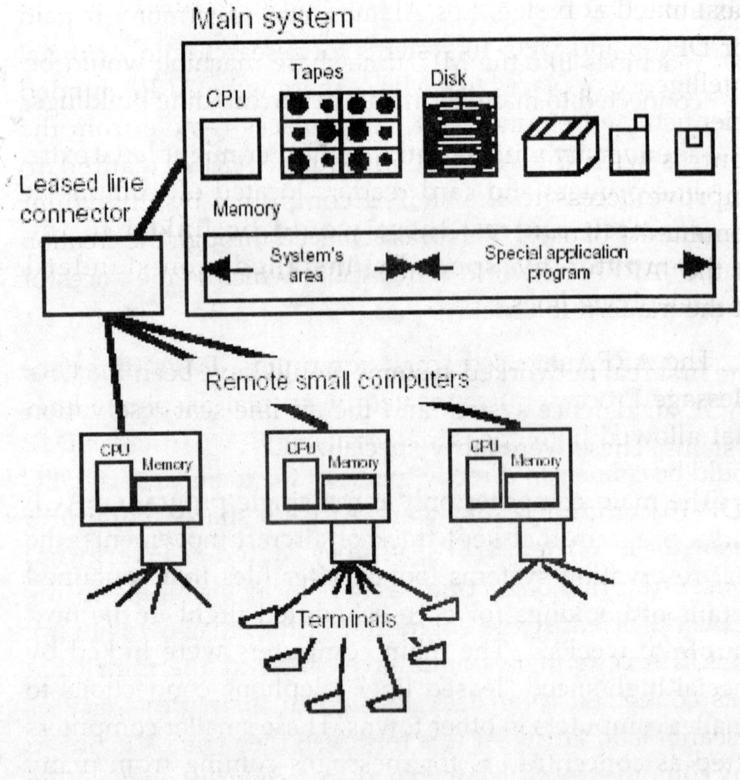

Figure 17

Early networked system, such as the airline seat reservation systems.

The remote computers joined via special telephone lines just provided input data for transactions. But, a much more innovative scheme for networking appeared around 1968. The US Department of Defence (DOD) sponsored a lot of research at universities and research institutes through its "Advanced Research Projects Agency" (ARPA). DOD-ARPA paid for large CDC computers for scientific computing at labs. like Oak Ridge, Los Alamos, and Livermore. It paid for DEC-6 and DEC-10 systems for research into Artificial Intelligence at places like MIT. There were ARPA funded scientists and engineers at many places remote from the centres with the ARPA computers. ARPA wanted to improve access to the shared computers by this wider community of users. This was achieved through the creation of the "ARPA network" (ARPAnet), which is the ancestor of the modern Internet.

The ARPAnet used small computers, IMPs (Interface Message Processors) connected by special telephone lines that allowed high speed data transfers. A particular IMP could be connected directly to one of the main CDC or DEC PDP-10 computers that were ARPA's shared computer resources. Other IMPs simply acted as terminal concentrators, connecting several local terminals to the network. Scientist and engineers, who were allowed to use an ARPA computer, would have access to a terminal that was connected to an IMP located in their university or research laboratory. At this terminal, they could "login" to any computer on which they had an account --- e.g. RLOGIN HOSTNAME=MITDEC10 USER=WILENSKY. If login was permitted, the chosen host computer would send a response message back to the IMP with details of the job that had been started for the new user. The IMP would record the details - "user on terminal 3 @ me connectedto job 20 on host MITDEC10." Subsequently, each line typed by the user was packaged by the IMP.

A packaged message had address details as well as the user's data e.g. if the user entered a "dir" command to list a file directory, the IMP would create a message like "3,IMP16,20,MITDEC10,dir" (terminal 3 @ me to job 20 @

MITDEC10, content 'dir'). An IMP didn't keep open a permanent connection to a remote host. Each message between user and host computer would be routed individually. Each IMP had a map of the network and the IMPs exchanged messages that described current traffic on links and identified areas with congestion. Using this information, an IMP could determine which link to use to forward a message. An IMP that received a message would check whether it should deliver it to a local host machine or forward it. Messages were stored in the IMPs until there was an opportunity to forward them across the next link. A message would make hops from IMP to IMP until it arrived at its destination. The message would be taken by the host, and the contents delivered to the user's job. Output from the job would be packaged by the local IMP. The response message would work its way back through the network, the return route might differ from the original route. The original intent of the ARPAnet was simply to provide this fairly flexible "remote login service" so that expensive ARPA computers could be shared by users all over the US. Very soon additional uses were found. As well as having accounts and file allocations for individual users, most computer OSs have some form of "group accounts"; a systems administrator can add an individual user to any number of these groups.

Once the ARPA net was running, researchers located at different places in the US could form a "group" on a particular research computer and work on shared files. Many found that the easiest way to contact their coworkers was to leave messages in shared files (avoiding problems with nobody answering phones, difficulties of different time zones etc). This kind of messaging lead to primitive "electronic mail" (email) systems. These mailing systems were regularized. Each user of a given host machine was allocated a "mail box" file; other users could append messages to this file. News services started about 10-15 years later. Within a few months of its establishment, the ARPA net went international making use of a telecommunications link via one of the first geostationary satellites to link up with a European subnetwork.

Starting with just a few machines in the late '60s, the ARPAnet grew to several hundred machines by the late 1970s, several thousand machines by the late 1980s (with a name change to Internet - it went between other more localized networks) and now the network has thousands of machines. Nowadays, most host machines manage without IMPs, doing message packaging and routing for themselves. In the mid-1970s, different types of computer network started to appear. By this time, computers were much less costly; and while it was common for an organization to have a large "mainframe" machine, this would be supplemented by a large number of "minicomputers" of various forms. Each minicomputer would have some disks, a display screen and keyboard, but they typically wouldn't all have printers, tape units etc.

Organizations set up "local networks" that simply joined up the different computers in any one office or department so as to allow them to share things like printers, and have some shared files. These shared file systems allow individuals working on different minicomputers to work together on a large project. These networks use messages to pass data in way somewhat similar to the widearea networks. For example if a user at one minicomputer typed in a command that specified that a file was to be copied from a local disk to a shared disk on another computer, the operating system on the mini would exchange messages with the computer that controlled the shared files; the first few messages exchanged would create the new file, subsequent messages would copy the existing file chunk by chunk.

The message passing mechanism was rather different from that used on the wide area networks. There are a variety of local network schemes ("token ring", "ethernet") with ethernet being currently the most popular. All the computers on an ethernet are connected to something like a co-axial cable. Messages are "broadcast" on this cable. All the computers can read messages at the same time, but only the computer to which a message is addressed will actually deal with the data. Modern personal computers typically have hardware interfaces and software in their operating systems that allow them to be connected to "ethernet" style networks. Each individual ethernet network has to be limited in size, but different local networks can be joined together by "bridges" and "routers" that can forward messages from one network to another. (A bridge or router serves much the same purpose as an ARPAnet IMP; it is a simple computer that runs a program that organizes the forwarding of messages.) Often local networks will have "bridges" that connect them to the worldwide Internet.

Modern Systems

The operating systems written for the mainframe computers of the late 1960s and early 1970s did succeed in delivering efficient CPU usage through "multiprogrammed batch computing", as well as supporting interactive timesharing. But these systems were often difficult to use (the "job control language", JCL, statements that had to be written to run a job were hard for the average user to understand, and the job control mechanisms were quite limited). The systems were proprietary; each computer manufacturer supplied an operating system for their computers, but these different operating systems were quite different in their styles of JCL and the facilities that they provided. Such differences hindered those users who had to work with more than one kind of computer. Further the code for these OSs was often poor. Most of the systems had not been designed, they had just grown. More and more features would have been added to an original simple multiprogrammed OS. Consequently, the systems were difficult to maintain.

Modern operating systems started to appear in the 1970s. Their designers had different objectives. With hardware costs declining, there was no longer a need to try to maximize machine usage. Some computer power could be "wasted" if this made the system easier to use and so made the users more productive. Unix was one of the first of the modern systems; its designers sought to create a system that would make programmers more productive. Later systems, like the Macintosh OS, have focussed on the needs of other less sophisticated users.

UNIX

Unix started to be developed around 1969, with the first published description appearing in 1973. It was developed at an ATT research lab. and was made freely available to universities, encouraging its widespread adoption. Unlike earlier operating systems which had been written in assembly language, the code for Unix was largely in C. The use of a high level language made the code much easier for programmers to understand and maintain. Further, the Unix OS was designed! The programmers who developed Unix started with a clear idea of how their OS was to work and what services it was to provide. Unix was more limited in its aims than many other OSs of the time. It was intended solely to provide a good environment for timeshare style program development. Other OSs were attempting to do timesharing, and database transactions, and run large jobs, and ...; but such different uses of a computer tend to conflict resulting in poor performance in all areas. The design for Unix modelled the OS in terms of several layers (when describing the design, someone made an analogy with a nut or an onion and introduced terms like" kernel", "shell" etc --- these names have stuck):

— the innermost layer (the "kernel") has the code for the i/o handling routines ("device drivers") etc;

— another layer contains the code for process management, file management, and memory management;

— further layers contain code for looking after wide area and local networks and so forth;

— the next layer out comprised large numbers of useful utility programs -programs for copying files, comparing files to find differences etc

— the outermost layer (the "shell") was the job control language interpreter, but this JCL interpreter was much more flexible than any that had been proposed previously.

Unix was originally written for a particular kind of computer (the "PDP11/20") manufactured by Digital Equipment Corporation (DEC). But, the relatively clean design of the system, and the use of a high level language, made it possible for the system to be adapted to other computers (only the "device drivers" and other really low level code had to be redone). Unix was moved to related but more powerful computer architectures (DEC's VAX series of computers) and to totally different computer architectures. During the 1980s, Unix was adapted to run on computers as diverse as the modern Cray supercomputers down to personal computers with Intel-80386 CPU chips. The US Department of Defence's Advanced Research Projects Agency (ARPA) sponsored development of Unix at the University of Berkeley. The Berkeley developers added features to support virtual memory and networking (both wide area and local networking). Late in the 1980s, many computer companies, ATT, Berkeley University, IEEE, etc got together and established standards for all Unix systems. Unix thus has the advantage of being a system that is non-proprietary, is widely available, and is effective in its original role of supporting program development.

Most students continuing with computing studies will eventually get to work with some Unix systems. Modern Unix systems have been expanded so as to handle tasks other than the "programmers' workbench" of the original design. These extensions (to handle large databases, some transaction processing and so forth) were demanded by customers. In some respects, these extensions detract from Unix which no longer has a quite the simplicity and elegance of its early forms.

Macintosh OS

The Macintosh OS, and things like Windows 3, represent more modern operating systems, having evolved in the ten to fifteen years after the start of Unix. The important ideas in the Mac OS (and later systems meant to work in similar style) were developed at Xerox's Palo Alto Research Centre during the 1970s and early 1980s (Apple started the Mac OS by getting a licence to use Xerox's ideas). Starting around 1972, Xerox PARC had had a project that aimed to explore what the "office of the future" would be like. Obviously, the office workers were going to make heavy use of computers. The Xerox researchers realized that the old systems were inappropriate.

The old systems had the computer as sort of oracle, surrounded by priests (the system's programmers and system's administrators) and neophytes (the computer operators); even the newer Unix systems had to have "system's gurus" to attend them and keep users at bay.

In an "office of the future", individual's would have their own computers, and these therefore would have to have operating systems that did not need priestly ministrations from gurus or others. Unlike other developers of that period, the Xerox group realized that the cost of CPU power was going to drop dramatically. Consequently, it wasn't going to be important to keep the CPU efficiently employed, what was going to be important was the efficient use of time of the office workers. So it was going to be worthwhile "wasting" CPU cycles with the computer doing extra work if this would simplify the tasks of the user.

Given these premises, the Xerox group focussed on what they thought would be the needs of users; they identified factors such as:

— visual displays for "high-bandwidth" communication (show the user what programs and files are available for use etc);

— direct manipulation (use of mouse pointer, selection of object represented visually [as an "icon"], picking a command from a menu - the "point-andclick" interface rather than the "remember-and-type-command" interface of Unix and older systems);

— consistency (every program working in a similar manner);

— intercommunication (e.g. easy transfer of pictures, text and other data between programs).

Xerox developed a variety of experimental systems embodying the features that they felt would empower users and make computers more useful. However, Xerox never really brought these experimental systems to the level of practical, affordable products.

Steve Jobs and others at Apple in the early 1980s recognized the importance of the Xerox ideas and worked to make them practical. The Mac OS of 1984 was the first system that could really deliver computer power to all users.

4

Online Teaching

The need to educate a large and varied population in English as the lingua franca in South East Asia has given rise to a number of problems, which are in a general sense also faced in the teaching and learning of other types of knowledge and skills. One of the most serious problems is the unhappy force-fed pedagogy in which many teachers and students find themselves trapped.

The teaching and learning practices based on 'teaching to the exam', common in many Hong Kong public and private institutions, are becoming increasingly suspect, but because of the need for the face validity that norm-referenced standardized assessment promises, these practices continue. Internet technology, which could potentially resolve this situation, is instead often forced to serve the same outmoded and dehumanizing educational models. While this problem is most keenly felt at primary and secondary levels, even tertiary education is not free of it. One of the most serious shortcomings of these practices is that they habitually result in students merely learning how to parrot formulae. Students frequently do not learn how to apply to real world situations the formulae they are compelled to memorize at school. In the case of language learning - sometimes through no fault of the teachers, who are often themselves victims of the pressure to teach for short-term gains - this may consist of drilling 'set phrases', which are made to substitute for grammatical and communicative competence in the language.

The information that is passed on to students is often a legacy of several generations of pedagogy, and, in addition to becoming quickly outmoded, is often degraded in the process of transmission (e.g., the 'set phrases' taught at school may not be relevant to real world communication). Regardless of how one accounts for problems in language education, there are clearly serious deficiencies in the quantity and quality of English courses (even in relatively prosperous regions such as Hong Kong). This is true whether the courses are based on brick (i.e., face-to-face) or 'click' (i.e., online) models.

The College of Life Long Learning (CL3), HKUST, to produce online 'workplace English' courses for professionals, and 'bridging' courses for secondary school-leavers who have been out of school for a number of years and who wish to enroll in tertiary courses. Both groups are mainly Cantonese-speakers at a wide range of English proficiency levels, who require a broad array of receptive and productive English skills. It was not immediately apparent how current multimedia technologies could be employed to develop and deliver high-level interactive online language learning content. Despite the Web's potential to provide courses on demand, most content delivery systems still offer an unsatisfactory range of activity types and learning options for dynamic language learning. It was determined that the overall design principals of a system for the creation and online delivery of language courses should at least aim at addressing some of the major logistic problems in education, by:

— appealing to a wide range of learner proficiencies and interests;

— motivating low-proficiency students, who often suffer from low self-esteem, to engage in high-level interaction;

— providing quality, individualized instruction to a large number of varied learners 'on the fly';

— ensuring a coherent, planned and progressive curriculum, and the transmission of core information, while also providing opportunities for self-discovery, problem solving, collaboration, creativity and the pursuing of individual learning paths;

— freeing and enabling the teacher to act more often as a mentor, and less often as a pedagogue;

— allowing materials developers and instructors - who often have limited technical knowledge and resources - to create engaging and meaningful communicative, collaborative and problem solving activities;

— integrating intrinsic, criterion-referenced and performance-oriented formative assessment into the learning process, thereby minimizing the need for extrinsic, norm-referenced summative assessment;

— providing quicker and more reliable reporting to the instructor (and allowing for easier grading), and also more effective and quicker feedback to learners; and

— allowing assessment of the content by the students.

It was also of course important that the system allow for the specific pedagogical needs of language courses. This meant implementing opportunities for students, who may have little perceived need or chance to use the target language in their daily lives, to gain accuracy and fluency in all skill areas. This includes authentic listening and speaking activities (e.g., a mechanism for listening to and recording simulated telephone conversations for study and assessment), as well as writing and reading activities (e.g., vocabulary acquisition aided by an online lexical database, and access to a range of online reference tools, such as dictionaries, encyclopedias and thesauruses).

While Internet technologies potentially allow for a highly interactive educational model (e.g., through retrieval of online data, as well as interaction among students and with the instructor), there is often a tension in the institutional need for high-throughput (often, in online delivery, this is couched in terms of 'scalability'). In the absence of reliable, affordable and easily implemented Artificial Intelligence systems for language acquisition by human beings (e.g., natural language parsing), this dilemma requires the careful preparation of objectively scored activities - ideally aimed at 'higher-order' outcomes, as well as the development of collaborative activities that make minimal demands on instructor input, monitoring and feedback. Equally important, the activities, content and technologies must fit the learners' needs and learning styles, which in this case are extremely varied.

Several currently available course delivery systems were evaluated, and while all permit information delivery and assessment, none applied the particular mechanisms for language learning suggested above. Also, most systems leave much to be desired in the ease with which content can be authored, the degree to which individual learners can be accommodated, and social interaction encouraged. Internet technologies continue to make available new expanded forms of communication that take time to be integrated into existing course delivery systems, and most of these systems do not allow easy incorporation of new technologies. It was decided that database-driven Internet technologies have matured to the extent that it is feasible to develop an original, customizable Web-based delivery system tailored to specific needs, which can be used to create and deliver interactive online content and to manage online courses.

Other parameters set for this system were that it must allow courses to be undertaken through a series of sequenced activities and units, though with a high degree of flexibility in the sequencing (i.e., learners are generally expected to complete a 'unit' within a set period, but may elect a different sequence than that recommended). It must allow for branching so that more able learners (or learners with different academic or job-related needs) can pursue different learning paths and activities within the same course. It must, furthermore, allow the creation of both objective, automatically-graded as well as open-ended activities, which are common to most learning 'platforms' and which are useful, for example, in reading and listening comprehension, essay submission, etc. Less conventionally, it must allow sequenced access by learners (via 'Voice over Internet Protocol' - VOIP technologies) to asynchronous voice discussion Web boards. The remainder of this paper illustrates yet another, even less conventional activity type implemented in an online English course currently driven by this system, viz, a tool that learners can use to create and post role-plays on the Web.

Online Role-plays

Education is an admirable thing. But it is well to remember from time to time that nothing that is worth knowing can be taught.

While not necessarily negating the role of the instructor, most academics accept that 'higher' levels of learning, such as 'critical thinking', are the preferred outcomes of the educational process. There is constant concern about whether universities are producing students capable of achieving the higher order learning outcomes listed in Bloom's taxonomy of educational objectives (i.e., recall comprehension application analysis synthesis evaluation). The term often used by linguists to describe advanced communicative proficiency is 'pragmatic competence', which includes the ability to critically evaluate what is said or written and to respond in a culturally appropriate manner (the 'language culture' may be defined by international social, academic or professional norms).

One way such outcomes are being encouraged is through role-playing activities, whether face-to-face or at a distance. These are being used in almost every discipline, including such unlikely subjects as Accounting. Many online projects have emerged that use 'virtual worlds' and personally assigned avatars for educational role-playing. The benefits of role-playing for generalized educational settings are detailed in Jones, and specifically for language learning in, e.g., Ladousse; Crookall and Oxford; and Bambrough.

The course delivery system described above incorporates a role-playing activity that makes it possible for students easily to manipulate animated characters on screen, assign them gestures and body language, develop narrative lines and write dialogue that is synthesized and 'spoken' by the characters, whose mouths move synchronously with the dialogue. This 'scripting tool' encourages language learners to use idiomatic grammar, appropriate vocabulary, sentence stress etc. Students are supplied copious amounts of authentic, comprehensible input for this activity. They can listen while the text they wrote is read back to them, and thus hear standard pronunciation (they can also select any material on the site for synthesis).

The learners recognize that the synthesized stress, rhythm and intonation are not entirely human, but they report finding the relatively high accuracy in pronunciation useful. This activity has the benefit of allowing students to compose written text while practicing spoken communication. Scarcella and Crookall review research to show how simulation facilitates second language acquisition by giving students the opportunity to try out new language in a safe environment. Three learning theories which they discuss claim that learners acquire language when:

— they are exposed to large quantities of comprehensible input through being engaged in genuine communication as part of the roles assigned to characters,

— they are actively involved in worthwhile, absorbing interaction, which tends to make students forget they are learning a new language, and

— they experience positive feelings and attitudes.

These studies claim that the simulation of 'real-life' problems helps students develop their critical thinking and problem-solving skills. Role-playing would certainly appear to be useful to the extent to which we view language as a vehicle for the realization of interpersonal relations and social transactions. The role-playing activity in this system allows students to practice and demonstrate 'higher-order' linguistic skills such as the pragmatic devices necessary for developing a narration, resolving a conflict, conducting a negotiation, etc., while also being a useful vehicle for practice in basic grammar, vocabulary and conversational language devices. Students who are normally shy to speak spontaneously in a classroom because of concern about their imperfect English say they appreciate the opportunity to practice using language in this context.

The activity gives students the opportunity to express cultural values and to be creative, while also developing practical scenarios for business and social communication. Another serendipitous benefit of the activity is that it appears to give students who have limited technology fluency more confidence in the use of computer applications. Incidentally, it also appears less prone to plagiarism: students seem less inclined to copy holophrastically from other sources when they are scripting for the digital puppets. The activity was designed to make it possible for students to work collaboratively at a distance, and while role-playing may be an ideal participatory exercise in active learning, this ideal may not be fully realizable for students who find it difficult to schedule online meetings in order to co-design plays.

Most students who have taken the course to this point are professionals looking to improve their English, and they have chosen to use this activity to design individually written, rather than collaboratively written role-plays. The students nevertheless still socialize through the public 'production' of their plays and through classmates' feedback, as well as in the virtual relationships between the animated characters. Several of the higher-order outcomes that are claimed for team-based role-playing activities are also possible from individual role-plays, such as increased confidence in language production, heightened discriminatory skills, and the sheer fun that comes form the act of personal expression and creation.

Some collaborative elements are retained even when the students do not work together: in addition to commenting on and grading each others' plays (by assigning 'stars'), many students have spontaneously carried on narrative lines from other students' plays. The students are given considerable language input and practice before each role-play activity (which are assigned once in each unit, or sometimes in alternative units).

A thematic context is developed in each unit, and relevant grammar and lexis is provided through a variety of interesting and interactive activities - including via (licensed) popular songs streamed from our server. This language input is very different than that normally made available in the classroom, and is based on extensive research into the language learning difficulties of the students. The students are also encouraged to use a 'concordancing tool' to look up authentic usage in relevant corpora of online texts. The students' instructors give encouraging and detailed feedback after each role-play, which the students can re-write. The purpose and structure of the role-plays is made clear to the students, otherwise the benefits of such communicative methods may not be perceived by those students who are used to conventional lecture and essay assignment methods.

The system outlined in this paper allows language teachers and materials writers to take advantage of recent advances in Internet technology (e.g., multimedia, text retrieval, and database support) to deliver instruction and encourage participatory learning for 'higher-order' outcomes. The online English course developed on this system seeks to address the cognitive and affective language-learning needs of particular learners. One modality the system makes possible is the pairing of computer animation and speech technology in order, for example, to encourage language learners to experiment with manipulating the second language in social or business contexts, according to their own particular goals. The role-playing exercise described in this matter is the most popular activity in the online English course: 98% of students found it 'very interesting'. Our overriding and continuing goal in the development of this system and the courses it supports is to pursue responsible innovation driven by our students' needs.

Quality Assurance in Online Teaching

E-teaching and E-learning have grown exponentially in the past few years. By December 1999, about half of the universities and colleges in the United States offered courses through the Internet or videoconferencing. E-teaching and E-learning have become major themes in education. To support these activities, many online self-paced tutorials have been created as part of an online course or as the sole component of a course. It is crucial to develop high quality online tutorials. There are five quality-assurance strategies that tutorial creators can use to guarantee a high quality tutorial: project management, best-practice benchmarking, user-needs assessment, usability testing, and formative evaluation.

The ILT is designed to help students develop skills to search, locate, evaluate, and use information effectively in their life-long learning. It consists of six modules: (1) Exploring the Library; (2) Library Online Catalog I; (3)

Library Online Catalog II; (4) Finding Periodical Articles; (5) Searching the WWW; and (6) Evaluating & Citing Sources. Its target audience is first-year undergraduates at HKUST.

First-year undergraduates are required by their Schools to participate in Library orientation. Previously, the orientation consisted of a walking tour of the library and a hands-on library class held in the Library Computer Lab. The tour helped students familiarize themselves with the facilities, collection, and services of the library. The class showed students how to search for information in the library catalog and databases effectively. To offer students an alternative way of learning, the library created the ILT for self-learners. Students can either join a tour and a class, or they can learn from the ILT on their own. In either case, students are required to take the quizzes on the ILT to show that they understand the key points presented in the six modules. Our library began to design the first three modules in March 2000 and completed them in August 2000. Modules 4 - 6 were started in October 2000 and released in February 2001. The appendix "Designing Online Tutorials with WebCT: A Flow Chart" summarizes all the key steps we took in producing and managing the ILT. The quality-assurance strategies used in the process are discussed below.

The ILT is targeted at about 1,900 first year undergraduates. Designing and managing an online tutorial for that many students is an "uphill task". Without proper project management techniques, chaos might reign. The two most important methods were the project management web site and the timetable.

Project Management Web Site

The web site "Information Literacy Tutorial for New

Students" tied together everything related to the project. It helped maintain a clear direction and facilitate communication among the project members. By keeping this working document up-to-date, we had a time-saving strategy since everything related to the project (proposal, style guide, students' comments, etc.) could be found on the site easily and quickly.

Developing the Timetable

Time Management is critical to the success of any project. We tried to set realistic deadlines for various stages of the project and to adhere to them.

Learning by borrowing from the best and adapting their approaches to fit your own needs is the essence of benchmarking.

What are Best Practices?

Best practices are documented strategies employed by highly acclaimed companies. A simple definition for best practices could be "excellent ways of doing something, a product, an online tutorial, etc."

We posted a question on BI-L (a global online discussion group on library instruction that has about 3,000 members) asking for online tutorials created on WebCT, i.e., the courseware we decided to use for designing our tutorial.

Quality Instruction Programs of Libraries

We examined the instruction programs of award winners and major university libraries from around the world which yielded fruitful results.

Searching and browsing key information-science journals helped us locate excellent online tutorials. We also used search engines to mine relevant tutorials.

After trying out and comparing a number of online tutorials, we learned what best-practice benchmarks were. We then followed these benchmarks when producing our own tutorial. This exercise spared us the problem of re-inventing the wheel and shortened the development time tremendously. It ensured our tutorial was in line with the best tutorials available.

Learning from Bad Examples

Not every online tutorial examined was of good quality. Some were poorly designed and caused a lot of problems for their users. These bad examples taught us what to avoid when designing our tutorial.

User Needs Assessment

Online tutorials are meant for users, not designers. Therefore, the tutorial should be user-centered rather than designer-centered. Unfortunately, quite a few tutorials we examined were designer-centered and users would find them difficult to use, or even useless. The first step in designing a user-centered tutorial is to learn the needs of the target user group. We assessed our users' needs for the tutorial in two ways:

We brainstormed on Module 1 (introduction to library services, facilities, and collection) by asking colleagues from Circulation and Library Reserve to give us ideas on what should be included in the module. They have frequent contact with first-year undergraduates and understand the needs of these students very well. Their contribution was substantial.

Second- and third-year students know (or wished they knew) what they needed when they were in their first year.

We interviewed nine of these students. The interview was divided into two parts: (1) Soliciting free thoughts from the students, and (2) Prompting students' ideas by showing them a tentative proposal of the three modules and asking them what they considered important for first-year students. We asked the students whether there were any important items missing from the proposed modules.

Usability Testing

These are studies designed to examine how usable a product is. The product can be anything: a software program, a web site, or an online tutorial. The goal is to improve the usability of the product.

Usability studies help create a truly usable (user-friendly) product. As Susan Fowler said: "Probably the best reason to test for usability is to eliminate those interminable arguments about the right way to do something. Your design team can go around in circles for years without finding the right solution to an interface problem... With human-factors input and testing, however, you can replace opinion with data. Real data tends to make arguments evaporate and meeting schedules shrink."

Most computer-related companies have at least one usability lab. See these examples, Microsoft's usability lab and NCR's usability lab. Some libraries such as Yale University Library conduct usability tests as well.

One of the most popular and important usability studies is the "think aloud" method (more commonly called Usability Test). It observes and analyzes user behavior with a product or a product prototype. It comprises five key components:

1. The goal: to improve the usability of a product
2. Testers represent real users
3. Testers do real tasks
4. User behavior and commentary are observed and recorded
5. Data is analyzed to uncover problems. Corrections are then recommended HKUST Library's Usability Study The usability test for Modules 1-3 employed two groups of testers: a "think-aloud" group and a self-paced group. The think-aloud group had five students and each of them was asked to "think aloud" while "test-driving" the tutorial. A project team member observed the student and noted down problems that s/he encountered. The self-paced group consisted of fifteen students who went through the three modules on their own and emailed us their comments.

Mix of the Student Testers

Most of the 20 students were undergraduates from Years 1 to 3 and were in different departments. A few were postgraduate students. We preferred undergraduate students since the tutorial was designed for them. The postgraduate students were invited in the hope that their more "mature" ideas would help improve the tutorial. The testers were equally divided between male and female. The 20 students were a good mix and offered different opinions.

Usefulness of the Usability Test

The usability test results revealed our ILT had plenty of room for improvement. Here is one example. Originally there was a message on the final page of each module:

"Please return to and take thefor this module." Many students repeatedly clicked on the two logos as if they were hyperlinks. By replacing the icons with text, we eliminated the problem.

The "think-aloud" group helped us identify more problems than the self-paced group. Although this method was more time consuming, it was more rewarding. Therefore, when we conducted the second usability test for Modules 1 to 3, we only adopted the "think aloud" method.

The Second Usability Test

The second usability test for Modules 1 to 3 served as an important evaluation before the ILT was implemented. Five new first-year students signed up for the test. We excluded students from other years because new first-year students represented the real users of the tutorial.

Formative Evaluation

This is a process that evaluates a product from start to finish. In other words, you start evaluating your product while you are creating it. If you evaluate your product when it is completely finished, you may find it too late to make any effective modifications. For Modules 1 to 3, we went through five stages of formative evaluation: initial evaluation, design evaluation, content evaluation, product evaluation, and implementation evaluation.

By applying these five methods of quality assurance (project management, best-practice benchmarking user-needs assessment, usability testing, and formative evaluation), we achieved our goal of producing a highly usable online tutorial. Students' comments have confirmed our belief that the tutorial is indeed user-friendly and useful. For the past two years, over 1,000 first year students have tried the tutorial by early October. Over 80% of those who filled out the evaluation said that they would recommend the tutorial to others. One wrote:

> "The [Information Literacy Tutorial] modules help me to revise what I've learned and enhance my skill. I'm very pleased with how UST librarians made the modules and set the quizzes. It made me feel that the staff here are serious about academic studies. This gives me confidence in studying at this University, and now I feel I start to love UST!!"

To maintain the high quality of the ILT, we constantly review and update it by incorporating the newest possible technologies and the latest development in information literacy.

The government of Hong Kong also promotes the employment of IT in education. As early as 1998, Joseph W.P. Wong, the Secretary for Education and Manpower, suggested increasing the effectiveness and the quality of teaching and learning through the use of IT in education. To achieve this target, a five-year strategy has been formulated.

According to the strategy, professional and technical support for schools and teachers will be set up whilst about 100 secondary schools were to have their own multi-media learning centers by the year 2000. The Chief Executive, in his 1999 Policy Address entitled "Quality People, Quality Home", also announced that the government has already allocated financial and manpower support for achieving the five-year strategy in promoting IT in education.

University education in Hong Kong is set up as an example to educators at primary and secondary levels. With limited resources and manpower compared to the universities, educators in primary and secondary levels try to learn from the experience of those using IT in university education. As a matter of fact, with the comparative advantage of resources and manpower, the level of IT use in university education is much greater than at other levels of education in Hong Kong. Some of the universities, such as the Chinese University of Hong Kong, the University of Hong Kong, and the Hong Kong University of Science and Technology, even conduct research on helping the implementation of IT at primary and secondary levels of education.

Nonetheless, as society now stresses the important of IT, everyone seems to be working hard on it without asking any questions. IT is just a 'hardcore' element and will not improve the quality of education unless we use it carefully and merge it with education. We may be able to get some of the picture from outside experience. For instance, not all lecturers are willing to employ IT in education due to their own characteristics and past experience in using computers. Some of them have already adopted the traditional way of teaching and they will consequently find it difficult to use IT in their teaching.

The reason is that if they have to employ IT in their teaching, it means that their way of teaching will probably change and they may not be able to cope with it. What is more, some of them may even find it not so easy to learn how to handle IT. They will spend a lot of time figuring out how to use, say, computer software, before they can prepare the course handout on the Internet. To them, it is time consuming compared with the effort of preparing the so-called traditional hardcopy handout. In addition, some may even think that their job security may be threatened if more and more IT is employed in education. For instance, they may think that if all the course materials are uploaded onto the Internet, then the university may not need them to conduct lessons.

In order not to employ IT in teaching, they may use different kind of reasons, such as the computers that they are using are too out-dated that they cannot meet the demands of IT-aided education. Besides, they will try to justify, and to a certain extent they are correct especially in the Hong Kong academic environment, that they are so busy with administrative and research work that they have no time for learning and using IT in their education. Second, students' technology skills and attitudes can also affect the success of IT implementation in education. It is almost meaningless using IT in education if students lack the technology skills to handle it or their attitudes are set against it. Luckily, most of the students in this generation can handle IT quite well and they are comfortable using it. Furthermore, students want their lecturers to use more IT in lessons. This is especially so, as illustrated by Walters and Necessary, to students at university for, as students grow up, their experience in using computers and IT becomes more sophisticated and they are more open to accept the use of IT in education.

Third, even though lecturers are willing to use IT in education, he or she may be prevented from using IT simply because of the lack of skills, lack of resources, or lack of time in developing related materials. In other words, they lack back-up support from their institution. As pointed out by Chiero and Takacs, Reed, Wells and Dombrowski, two important factors in making the lecturer adapt more easily to the use of IT are resources and group norms. Resources refers to time, training, and support. If the lecturer is provided with adequate time to develop IT in education, or if the time the lecturer uses in such development is recognized by the university, the lecturer is likely to employ, or at least will not resist, IT in education. Also, there are many different kinds of information technologies available in the market. The lecturer may not be able to tell which one is suitable for his teaching or not. Therefore, adequate training in the different kinds of IT or even teaching the lecturer how to use certain software will surely help the lecturer a lot in choosing which IT is suitable for his class.

In addition, lecturers may come across some difficult technical problems in handling IT when, say, hosting a Web course. If the problem cannot be solved or problems arise again and again, the eagerness of the lecturer in using IT in education may fade out. Thus, responsive support for the lecturer is also important for the success of IT use in education. Group norms are also important. If the norm of the division or even the university is so IT-oriented that teaching is widely support by Internet and / or audio-visual equipment, then the lecturer will most likely also use IT in his teaching as well, so as not to lag behind others. The creation of such group norms, however, is largely dependent on the effort of the division or the university in promoting the use of IT.

After viewing the issues of implementing IT in education, it is better for us to consider again the results of the implementation. Can implementation really achieve what we are targeting, i.e., raising the quality of education? The Chief Executive has said that the minds of educators in Hong Kong have changed in the sense that they have begun to accept the use of IT in education. However, is this really the case? Or, are they going in the right direction? Drawn from the previous discussion, the questions worth considering are, first, do lecturers really welcome or oppose the use of IT in teaching? Second, do students really enjoy learning after the employment of IT in education? Third, are there any factors, such as the attitude of the department, the university, or the personal characteristics or past experience of the lecturers in handling IT, that will help or hinder the development of the use of science and technology in education? Also, is the employment of IT alone (input from computers or the Internet, for instance) sufficient to raise the interest and level of educational achievement among students and lecturers?

In other words, are the video, audio or lecturer notes and course materials posted on the Web good enough to allow lecturers to claim that they have already used IT in their courses and that their students can benefit from it? Or, is it correct for the students to expect that the use of IT is making it easier for them to check their course information and obtain the lecture notes? If this is not the case, then what are the more appropriate paths that we should take and what factors should we take into consideration when employing IT in education for the sake of the next generation?

In the case of the universities in Hong Kong, can we detect the above situation? Even before the government started to promote the use of IT in education, some lecturers already employed the Internet to helping students. Nonetheless, from my own experience and observation, most of the lecturers only post the lecture notes and the like on the Web. Is it the case that the lecturers and the students using such Web materials are able to claim that they have already used science and technology in education or even in learning? If that is the case, then what is the essence of the employment of science and technology in education, especially at the university level? On the other hand, some of the universities are willing to use IT in their education. For instance, they would like to use some of the education platforms, like WebCT, in their teaching.

Yet, this does not mean that they can go on as they please. They still face some constraints. For instance, they may lack technical support and do not know how to handle software and hardware problems. Second, even the institution may not totally support them because it requires a lot of financial and manpower support. It also involves many complicated issues such as copyright. Third, they also fear that the departments and universities concerned will not recognize the time and effort they have put into using IT in education. Some of them, on the other hand, are against the use of IT for fear that they will lose their jobs.

In view of the above actual Hong Kong situation, then, what approach should the universities, lecturers, and policymakers concerned adopt in carrying out the promotion of IT in education? How can the universities and lecturers overcome these difficulties?

Literature reviews is part of the methodology for my study. We have tried to find some theories on implementing IT in education and tried to see how institutional or personal factors can help or hinder such development. Besides the literature reviews, we have also tried to get valuable information on the implementing of IT in some of the universities in Hong Kong by means of questionnaire. In mid-November, 2000, using email or direct contact, to professors in the Division of Social Science or related fields at the Hong Kong University of Science and Technology (total four samples) and the Hong Kong Baptist University (total four samples). Efforts were made, before the survey, to ensure that there would be normal distribution among the targeted interviewees in terms of position, age, and years of teaching experience, which I believe, may affect the neutrality of the samples. Thus, the sample contains professor, associate professor and assistant professor with varying years of teaching experience. The questionnaire is designed in the format of multiple choice, attitude test, and short questions, and is supposed to be finished within five minutes. The study acts as a pilot study.

In addition to that, with help from the Information Technology Service Center (ITSC) at the Hong Kong University of Science and Technology, results of a survey on student feedback on the use of IT in the University were analyzed for this study. After gathering the results from the questionnaire, I will analyze my data in quantitative and qualitative ways. In addition, we will try to show whether there are institutions or personal factors that help or hinder the use of IT in education. What is more, we will also use the literature and the theories of using IT in education and compare them with my findings to see whether universities in Hong Kong have similar experience in the implementation of IT in education.

The questionnaire response rate is 100% for the professors at the Hong Kong University of Science and Technology while there is only 50% response rate for the professors at the Hong Kong Baptist University. Among the responses, one is professor, two are associate professors, and two are assistant professors. The following are the brief summary of the findings: First, gender has little relevance to the willingness to use IT, namely the Internet, in university education. From the response, 66.67% are male while 33.33% are female. However, 25% of the male professors from our total of male respondents indicated that they do not use IT in their teaching. Also, 50% of the female professors indicated that they do not use IT in teaching. Thus, gender seems to have no relationship with the willingness among the professors to use IT in university education. In addition, years of teaching experience also had little relationship with willingness to use IT in university education. From the responses, 0% has less than two years of teaching experience.

A total of 33.3% have two to five years teaching experience. Also, 16.67% and 50% of the professors have six to ten and more than ten years of teaching experience respectively. However, 50% of the total respondents who have two to five years of teaching experience showed that they do not use IT in their university education. What is more, 33.3% of the total respondents who have more than ten years of teaching experience also indicated that they do not use IT in their university teaching. This shows that years of teaching experience, and age, can be regarded as having no relationship with the willingness of the professors to use IT in university education.

Male and female behave the same in facing IT and there is no gender difference. Another explanation for the finding that years of teaching experience has little relationship with willingness to use IT is that the professors are well educated and that the computer is not too difficult for them once they have made up their mind to learn it. From my study, over 50% of the respondents indicated that they have average or above-average knowledge in developing Internet materials. This shows that using the Internet for their teaching is not a difficult task for most of the professors. Concerning the years of teaching experience, my explanation is that whether they can accept new things and new technology compared with those that they have copied depends on the cognitive mind of the professors. As we have mentioned before, computer knowledge should not be difficult for them. The question is, are they ready to learn it? The degree of readiness, propose, is subject to whether the professor is open to new things or not and that may have no relationship with the years of teaching, or age, at all. Young professors can have a conservative mind while old professors may be very open. It really depended on the professor's personal characteristics.

Second, although 50% and 33.3% of the respondents indicated that they have some interest or a keen interest in developing Internet materials, professors use IT in their teaching for different purposes. Some of the professors used IT in their teaching as a means to gain promotion or recognition from the department and / or the university. From the study, 50% of the respondents showed that they have no idea on whether their effort in developing the Internet (no matter they have used it or not) will be recognized by the department.

Nonetheless, 33.3% of the respondents indicated that they think that their efforts in developing the Internet will be recognized by the department. This 33% also indicated that they have used IT in their university education. Thus, at least, it gives the impression that one of the reasons why these professors used IT in university education is to gain the university's recognition of their efforts for the sake of evaluation and promotion.

The explanation for this finding is that this may reflect the picture that some of the professors are not very eager to use IT in their teaching but nonetheless they do not resist it. They regard IT as a way of increasing their chances of promotion or getting a positive evaluation from the department. There is nothing wrong at all with this attitude and it may be positive to the development of IT in university education as well. The important thing is that at least they do not resist using IT in their teaching. In fact, we can expect that they will use it more and more once the university or the department concerned gives them adequate motive, such as recognition, rewards and so on.

Interestingly, from the study, 16.67% of the respondents that used the Internet in university education indicated they have an idea that their efforts in developing the Internet will not be recognized by the department. Also, the professors indicated that they used the Internet as a supplement to illustrate the point(s) and the idea(s) that cannot be covered during the lecture or to further illustrates the point(s) already taught in the lesson. In addition, the professor also stated that the Internet can also act as a means of allowing the students to self-explore the subjects by providing useful input from the World Wide Web to them. This gives the impression that the reasons for the professors using IT in university education are to facilitate teaching and for the benefit of the students.

However, we cannot classify the professors as simply self-interested and student-interest oriented. The professors use the Internet in their teaching also because they believe that the Internet can facilitate their teaching (25%), facilitate students' learning (75%), save time (25%), and so on. The professors used the Internet mainly as a way of letting students explore the subjects themselves (75%) and as a supplement or illustration for the lecturer (50% each).

Third, some of the professors, however, do not use IT in their university teaching. From the findings, 33.3% of the professors indicated that they do not use IT in teaching. Some indicated that there is a lack of manpower and financial support for the development of the Internet. Some also said that they do not use IT in university education because such development is time consuming and they lack the knowledge to do it. Some, however, indicated that they want to retain their teaching style and thus refuse to use IT in the university education. For this finding is that this reflects the fact that they find it difficult to adapt to new technology. This may be due to past experience or just because they cannot open their minds in accepting the new technology and change their teaching style.

There is nothing wrong in such a position and they may be good professors that only dislike using IT in teaching. However, in the IT age, it is the trend that they will be required to change. Such attitudes may create unnecessary confrontation and distrust between professors and university if the use of IT in university teaching becomes a fixed policy. Compromise and understanding should then be encouraged between the two parties. Also, the main difficulties that the professors faced when using IT in their teaching are lack of time and manpower support from the department and / or the university. Besides, 50% of them also indicated that another difficulty is the lack of manpower support from the department or the university. Other difficulties as identified by the professors in developing Internet materials also include the lack of financial support from the department or the university, lack of knowledge, and that their efforts are not recognized by the department.

Of professors who do not use IT in their teaching, all of them indicated that they may change their mind when there is enough manpower support provided by the department and / or the university and students have also made such demands. In addition, 50% of them also indicated that the university or the department must provide more financial support for them in order to develop Internet materials. Nonetheless, from the survey, we cannot see the effect of group norms on the use of IT in university education. This may be due to the fact that professors in Hong Kong act rather independently and are rarely affected by the group norm. However, it is still worth having a future study on this issue.

One of the implications of the study is that the successful implementation of IT in the university requires both the effort of the professors and the department and / or university. On the one hand, the professors cannot avoid the demands for changing their teaching style in order to enhance the quality of teaching. In fact, in the age of the so-called "information society", people will demand more access to the information. Students are not the exception. Thus, professors should be aware that their students will also demand a change in teaching style.

On the other hand, the university should also try its best to encourage professors, especially in terms of manpower and financial support, to use the Internet in their teaching. The main difficulty that the professors face in developing the Internet are lack of time, and lack of manpower and financial support from the university. Also, despite many positive results, 100% of the professors indicated that their workload increased after starting to use the Internet in their teaching. The need for more support from the university in developing Internet materials also shared by those professors who are not using the Internet in their teaching at present. Around 50% and 25% of the professors who are not using the Internet as part of their teaching would change their mind on condition that the university provided them more manpower and financial support in developing Internet materials respectively. By doing so, the benefit will finally go to the students. Nevertheless, we should bear in mind that IT, at least in university education, is not everything. It is true to say that IT can help us to work in an efficient way. Yet, IT itself can only guarantee, at most, the quantity but not the quality. To work in an efficient way does not mean that the work is being carried out in an effective way.

Nowadays, many professors use the Internet as a part of their university teaching. Some of them, however, use the Internet only to let students download the course lecture notes and related materials. This can help the teaching in an efficient way but it does not mean that the whole progress is made in an effective way. Therefore, we had better not lose ourselves entirely in IT. In addition, in implementing IT in university education, we should not neglect the need of our customers, that is, the students. That is to say, when we implement IT in university education, students should be, at least, the ones that benefit from such implementation. However, the question is, what is mean by "benefit"? Having a high access rate does not mean that the Internet is successful for teaching purposes and also does not mean that students can really benefit from the use of IT.

Maybe the instructor just uploads all the lecture notes onto the Web and requires the students to download them themselves. Students, therefore, have to access the course Web very often. Yet, this does not mean that the students benefit from such course Web. In accordance with a survey conducted by the ITSC at the Hong Kong University of Science and Technology, over 70% of the students showed that they are positive towards the use of IT in university education. Besides downloading the lecture notes, over 50%

and 70% of the students showed that they learned something from posting or reading the messages on the bulletin board by their classmates, instructor, or the teaching assistant respectively. Thus, when implementing IT, for instance the Internet, in university education, we should also cater for the needs and the interests of the students.

There are still some aspects that are not yet covered in this study. First, this study focuses mainly on the aspect of the professors and the university to see the main reasons for the difficulties in implementation of IT in university education. Nonetheless, the part of the students does not have much consideration in this study. As a matter of fact, the students in the university are one of the reasons why the implementation of IT is needed. Therefore, further study is needed on how the students view and respond to the implementation of IT in university education and what difficulties they are facing. Second, this study only focuses attention on the use of IT in university education. Yet, university education is just a part of the whole education progress.

Primary education, secondary education, special education, and even continuing education are also important. Primary education is said to be an important foundation for human development. Secondary education is also important for university education. Special education and continuing education are also important too. The use of IT here plays a different role and is also important. Thus, further study on the use of IT in these areas is needed. In addition, IT can apply to many different fields. Education is just one of them. We can also look into, for instance, the role of IT in the development of Hong Kong. Currently, the economy of Hong Kong is recovering. Yet, there are still many factors that endanger Hong Kong's leading economic position in the Asian region. Low salaries and strong competition are examples. It would appear that IT can help Hong Kong gain a competitive edge over other regions. Thus, it would be worthwhile conducting a further study on, for instance, how light industry in Hong Kong can make use of IT in production to gain a competitive edge. Such a study could, in return, help the government of Hong Kong to understand more about the economy of Hong Kong to make it easier for the government to formulate the appropriate policy. It is said that IT has become a part of our daily life.

Sometimes, however, we are so dependent on IT that when the computer, a part of IT, breaks down, say, due to the Y2K issue, the whole of society is affected. Thus, we also regard IT as a kind of risk to society. Some may suggest that it is better to depend on ourselves. Yet, in modern society it is hard for us to live without IT. Thus, it would be worthwhile conducting a further study on the issue of how we should achieve a balance between, on the one hand, relying on IT and, on the other, an appropriate risk perception in using IT.

Challenges and Guidelines for Online Learning Content

Hypertext is widely recognized to be a powerful medium for disseminating information. One of the prominent features of hypertext is that it is a type of non-sequential reading, from the readers' point of view. This contrasts with traditional text such as that in a book. There is no single order that determines the sequence of which piece of text is to be read.

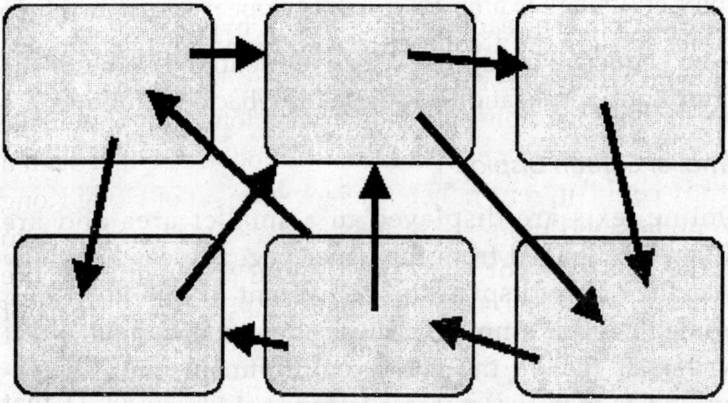

Figure 1: Non-sequential reading of Hypertext

Figure 1 shows a pattern of reading Hypertext. Readers are given the flexibility and choices of reading the text. Unlike reading conventional text, they do not need to read from the beginning to the end. However, also because of this flexibility, writers have to be more careful when designing the text, as they are no longer following the technique for writing conventional sequential text. Hypertext, while offering an entirely different approach to reading for the reader, also creates challenges for the writer. Raskin has mentioned, "Hypertext seems like a wonderful universally applicable, powerful, natural, human-oriented model for organizing and accessing knowledge...but when asked how the ends are made to meet...the designers become unspecific and waffle."

Potential Challenges in Writing Hypertext

Hypertext offers a degree of flexibility in reading pattern for the reader. At the same time, it has certain possible drawbacks. While the reader can decide what and how to read, the problems might be overchoice or overload of information; the reader getting lost in hyperspace as there is no sequence to follow. We have identified some of the causes and implications of these drawbacks as follows.

Smaller Screen Display

Online texts are displayed in a smaller area and are differently shaped from the paper page. Researches show that they only display the equivalent of one-third of a printed page at a time. Thirlway's reminder to online text writers is that in the online environment, more 'page-turning' is required, as most screens hold fewer (readable) characters than a page of a book. This is different from books because, in books, the reader can usually tell at a glance whether information is useful or not, whereas selecting and examining that same information on the smaller online display is more arduous (Landow from Horton 1990). Writers, therefore, have to decide what to put on a 'page', without letting readers lose critical information. They have to find an effective way to chunk the information to make it more readable.

Different Reading Habits and Behaviors online

In general, people seldom read online texts from the beginning to the end. They usually skim, scan, skip, flip, hop, and bounce just to look for what they want. In addition, they prefer short passages to long ones. Because of these factors, writers need to better organize their text and make navigation more easy and effective. Pieces of information should be linked in a clear and systematic way. Navigation and mapping techniques have to be carefully applied so that readers do not get lost in hyperspace.

Dropping Reading Speed Online

According to research, people's online reading speed decreases by about 39%. Thirlway has denied reading on screens as the best medium for reading. It is more tiring to read a screen than a page of a book. Therefore, writers sometimes have to use more simple and direct language to raise readability and make reading easier.

We have looked at the major feature of hypertext being a type of non-sequential reading and writing. We have also stated some of the possible challenges of designing and writing online materials. They are caused by:. smaller computer screen display; decreasing reading speed online and tendency of people to skip, scan and get tired more easily when reading online. We will try to summarize the guidelines from professional online text writers and my own experience, with the aim of providing our course developers with some hints on how to write effective Hypertext for learning content.

Guidelines for Writing Online Course Materials

We will summarize the guidelines from several aspects: length of text, which includes using chunking techniques and linking information; functions, referring to the organization and navigation of texts; and language, which covers clarity, consistency and preciseness.

Research suggests that in the hypertext environment, many short documents are preferable to a smaller number of long documents as people usually skip and scan and prefer shorter passages. For this reason, writers are advised to put the minimum of text on a page, with the information covering one subject only. The following figure illustrates the minimum of text:

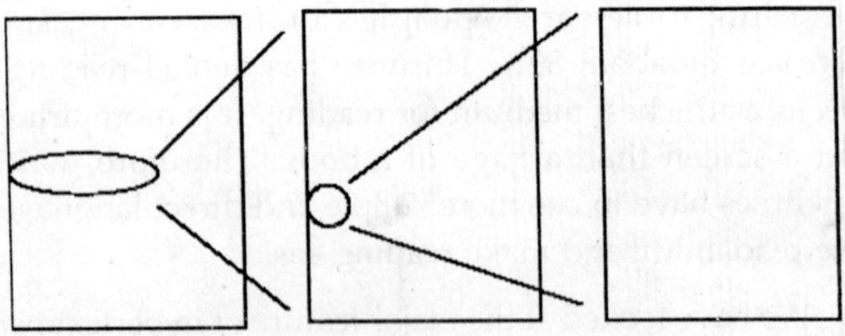

Figure 2: Minimum of Text

In Figure 2, the piece of text is displayed level-by-level. On the first page, only the list of sections is shown. The second page shows the contents of Section B, and the expanded point 3 is displayed on the third level/ page. In this way, readers can select what to read and focus on only one subject on each page.

Chunking

Chunking is breaking long pieces of texts into smaller 'self-contained' paragraphs. Writers are advised to write discrete topics, not sprawling passages. To help readers read more easily, headings and subheads can be used to label each chunk. In most cases, bullets are also useful as learning content appearing in note or point form is usually more readable when compared to long paragraphs.

Organization

In the early stage of course development, writers need to know the structure of their course in order to plan for expansion. To do this, they can plan the entire organization in advance, list all topics and even create dummy topics, insert links as they write even though they do not yet have the destinations. Hypertext systems can be hard and tricky to operate and follow. One of the misuses of Hypertext is that writers sometimes want to put a lot of information on the Web so they add a lot of links, which just makes it more overwhelming and difficult to read. We should, instead, keep it simple so that users do not have to learn too many ways of accessing the information

Experience has shown that readers expect the writer to blaze a trail for them. They like to be guided. Therefore writers can display the organization by adding a site map. The following is a course built on WebCT1 and it shows an example of a typical online table of contents displaying the organization.

Navigation

In the hypertext environment, readers can easily get trapped in vast hierarchies and networks of information. To prevent this, providing a navigation guide is important. Writers should give a clear starting point. One topic can be designated as the root or home topic. It should tell readers how the document is organized, and how to access the key topics. A table of contents can be presented to give readers the entire picture of the content. Links should be added in moderation. However, the appropriate number of links always depends on the nature and the content of the course. In some cases, we can provide a study guide or navigation guide to give information such as the essential requirements of the course, how to study the online course and where to get help etc.

Use of Language

For writing online course content, writers should try to

avoid using too much jargons, and too many acronyms and abbreviations. Some common examples are "booting", "FAQ", "FYI". Other than these, writers should also be cautious when using terminology, like "application", "button", "soft and hard copy", "drag", "enter", "window". These words have different meanings in the world of the computer and we should not assume that every learner is familiar with them.

Inconsistent language confuses readers. When writing online text, consistency of format, wording, and style should be maintained. For example, if we call it "the screen" in one place, do not call it "the monitor" somewhere else if referring to the same thing. It is important to keep it consistent because when phrasing, formatting, and displaying information consistently, readers can quickly learn the conventions used throughout the content. You can then rely on such conventions to make the content more concise and dependable. Examples for course development are words like

"Chapter", "Unit", "Topic"

· "the VDU", "the screen", "the monitor"

· "log on", "log in", "logon", "login", "sign in"

· "exit", "log out", "logoff", "quit"

People learning with computers expect the computer to speak directly and accurately. So writers should try to keep syntax simple and edit for short clear text to raise readability.

Table 1: Review of Main Ideas

Challenges for Writing Hypertext	*Guidelines for Writing*

	Readable Hypertext
Smaller Screen Display	Minimum of Text Chunking
DifferentReading Habits and Behavior Online	Organization Function
Dropping Reading Speed Online	Clarity of Language Consistency of Language Preciseness of Language

We have tried to state the possible challenges faced by course developers in writing effective hypertext and making best use of it. We have also tried to summarize from literature and experience some of the guidelines for writing readable hypertext, with the hope of raising the awareness of online course developers. These guidelines may serve as reminders of some commonly known facts whose importance may have been overlooked. However, writers should always look at the nature and content of their course and write with flexibility.

5

Assessing Computer Conferencing

In the one-room schools that dotted the North American landscape during the pioneer era, the tasks of a skilled and dedicated teacher were challenging, to say the least. The teacher performed several functions. Obviously, she or he provided direct instruction - in all school subjects, to children in up to nine different grades! Perhaps less obvious, the teacher had to spend long hours designing and organizing the learning experiences of the children. This teacher function often included non-traditional activities such as lighting the potbellied stove on each frigid winter morning so that the school would be habitable when the students arrived.

A third teaching function that was very important in these pioneer schools was creating a community of learners by facilitating student-to-student discourse. It was obviously impossible for one teacher to provide constant direct instruction to twenty-five students in up to nine different grades. Most of the learning in the one-room school took place as children in one grade worked in a peer-learning group while the teacher was providing direct instruction to children in another grade. Frequently the teacher would assign "the big kids" - i.e., those who knew more about the subject - to help "the little kids," those who knew less about the subject. These various teaching functions are now being replicated in a new "pioneering" context, that of online learning, to which we now turn.

Teaching Presence in an Online Environment

There are two reasons why we begin a paper on teaching presence in a virtual environment with a look back at teaching presence in an earlier pioneering era. First, in the earlier, supposedly simpler era of the one-room schoolhouse, it was clear that the functions of a teacher were multi-facetted. In that more physical, more observable environment, it is easy to see the function of the teacher as consisting of three major roles: first, as designer of the educational experience, including planning and administering instruction as well as evaluating and certifying competence; second, as facilitator and co-creator of a social environment conducive to active and successful learning; and finally, as a subject matter expert who knows a great deal more than most learners and is thus in a position to 'scaffold' learning experiences by providing direct instruction.

Another reason for our reference to the experience of pioneer teachers in one-room schools is that it serves as an analogy to the time consuming and often frustrating experience of twenty-first century "pioneer teachers" in online learning communities. As was the case in the one-room schools in the early twentieth century, creating the necessary "warmth" in the pioneering virtual learning environments of the early twenty-first century takes considerable teacher effort. However, the imperfect tools of today are harbingers of easier and more ubiquitous online learning tools, just as the one-room schools of long ago have given place to modern, well-equipped schools in rural centers. The tasks of the online teacher as gleaned from the literature and our experiences as teachers of graduate level, online courses. It then introduces a technique for systematically analyzing the context of the text-based transcripts of those courses.

We expect that these tools will allow teachers to assess and then improve their own postings in online courses. We also expect that these tools can be used for research designed to test hypotheses or diagnose problems in online teaching. We conclude the paper with the preliminary results of our analysis of the transcripts from two graduate level teaching courses.

Teaching in online courses is an extremely complex and challenging function. Therefore, study of this multifaceted function requires an appropriate theoretical perspective that frames this particular research context. This is provided by the framework of our extended research project - the goal of which is to better understand teaching and learning via computer conferencing in a higher education context through the development of analytical and measurement tools that assess critical discourse in a community of inquiry.

Our research is based on a model of critical thinking and practical inquiry developed by Garrison, Anderson and Archer. This model is framed by a community of inquiry model and used to illustrate the multifaceted components of teaching and learning in a text-based environment. The three elements of this framework are: cognitive presence, social presence and teaching presence. Earlier papers have discussed methodology of transcript analysis, cognitive presence, and social presence in computer conferencing. In the current paper we examine the variable that is most directly under the control of teachers-the task of creating and sustaining "teaching presence" in a text-based computer conferencing context. In a transactional approach to education, consistent with traditional higher education values, the teacher is expected to assume certain responsibilities and fulfill an important role. Regardless of the mediated nature of the communication, "it is the teacher's responsibility to precipitate and facilitate learning that has purpose and is focused on essential concepts and worthwhile goals".

Fulfilling the complex responsibilities of a teacher necessitates sustained and authentic communication between and among teachers and students. While control must be shared and choices provided, the discourse must also be guided toward higher levels of learning through reflective participation as well as by challenging assumptions and diagnosing misconceptions. This collaborative construction of knowledge is a challenge that all educators face. However, it is made extraordinarily difficult when it is the educator's responsibility to design, facilitate, and direct learning online. For learning to occur in this lean medium of communication, dependent on written language only, a strong element of what we refer to as teaching presence is required. We will now turn to the task of defining with greater precision what teaching presence is and how it may be measured.

Classification of Teacher Roles in Computer Conferning

The initial classification of teaching presence proposed by the present authors consisted of three characteristics - design and administration, facilitating discourse, and direct instruction. A review of the literature related to online teaching provides support for this classification.

Our three categories of teaching presence can be mapped directly to previous work by other researchers (see Table 1). First, it is important to note that Berge categorizes four major functions of the online moderator. He adds a "technical" support role to the three we have itemized. However, while we acknowledge that providing technical assistance to students is currently an onerous function of the online teacher, like tending the prairie school stove, we believe that its importance will decrease as users become more experienced and as the tools of online learning become more intuitive and ubiquitous.

Paulsen and Mason also divide the educational moderator's role into three major responsibilities - organizational, social, and intellectual. The one area where we depart somewhat from these authors is in terms of how we construct and define the social aspects of an educational experience. We have separated out the purely social elements as a separate element of a community of inquiry and refer to (this distinct element) it as "social presence".

The creation of the social environment is the responsibility of students as well as teachers. In our model, only the social aspects of the teacher's messages that directly relate to the content contributions from the student are included in the teaching presence category. The corresponding characteristic from a teaching presence perspective is the role of facilitating discourse. Finally, we refer to the third function as "direct instruction" rather than Berge's "pedagogical" which, in its broadest sense, can refer to all three functions or to Paulsen and Mason's "intellectual" which does not necessarily denote teaching at all.

Table 1

Models of teaching roles in computer conferencing

Anderson et al	*Berge*	*Paulsen*	*Mason*
Instructional design and organization	Managerial	Organizational	Organizational
Facilitating Discourse	Social	Social	Social
Direct Instruction	Pedagogical Technical	Intellectual	Intellectual

Rossman's extensive research provides empirical support for these classification systems. Through the analysis of over 3000 student end-of-course evaluations from 154 university courses, Rossman found student comments and complaints clustered into three major groupings - teacher responsibility, facilitating discussions, and course requirements. These map to our categories of direct instruction, facilitating discourse, and design and administration, respectively. Finally Coppola, Hiltz and Rotter's qualitative interview research with 20 'virtual professors" identified affective, cognitive and managerial roles (changes) as major categories undergoing change through the teaching of online courses. Obviously these three match directly with our indicators of teaching presence.

Lists of hints and suggestions for conference moderators and online teachers have also been provided by many authors. However, these provide few, if any guidelines by which teaching presence characteristics can be measured or assessed. To achieve this goal we have developed a template and tool for assessing teaching presence. We have done this through the provision of indicators and examples that clearly describe and measure the concept of teaching presence.

Rossman's extensive research provides empirical support for these classification systems. Through the analysis of over 3000 student end-of-course evaluations from 154 university courses, Rossman found student comments and complaints clustered into three major groupings - teacher responsibility, facilitating discussions, and course requirements. These map to our categories of direct instruction, facilitating discourse, and design and administration, respectively. Finally Coppola, Hiltz and Rotter's qualitative interview research with 20 'virtual professors" identified affective, cognitive and managerial roles (changes) as major categories undergoing change through the teaching of online courses. Obviously these three match directly with our indicators of teaching presence.

Lists of hints and suggestions for conference moderators and online teachers have also been provided by many authors. However, these provide few, if any guidelines by which teaching presence characteristics can be measured or assessed. To achieve this goal we have developed a template and tool for assessing teaching presence. We have done this through the provision of indicators and examples that clearly describe and measure the concept of teaching presence.

Describing Teahching Presence

We define teaching presence as the design, facilitation, and direction of cognitive and social processes for the purpose of realizing personally meaningful and educationally worthwhile learning outcomes. Teaching presence begins before the course commences. as the teacher, acting as instructional designer, plans and prepares the course of studies, and it continues during the course, as the instructor facilitates the discourse and provides direct instruction when required. Through adequate teaching presence, formal learning that facilitates personally relevant and educationally defined outcomes is achieved. We do not wish to denigrate individual learning that occurs through independent or self-directed study.

However, it is only through active intervention of a teacher that a powerful communications tool such as collaborative computer conferencing, or cooperative learning becomes a useful instructional and learning resource. Identifying and quantifying the types of teaching presence interventions give us some clues to developing better support tools for pioneers of online education. Usually a formal distance education course consists of much more than dialogue between and among teacher and students and includes course readings, web explorations, exercises and individual and collaborative projects.

Teaching presence mediates all of these components, however we have initially only·used our analysis tools on the computer conferencing component of the course. We are grateful to the reviewer of this article who pointed out that the analysis of teacher presence could be extended to other components of the course and we invite subsequent researchers to follow through on this approach. Teachers and students come to conventional higher education having already learned well-defined roles through years of common educational background and experience in the formal education system.

During online learning this background and prior experience are less relevant to the context, which can invoke feelings of anomie. This forces teachers and students to explicitly define or redefine their functional roles. They must rely less on predefined roles and behavioral expectations. In addition, for the teacher "the ability to create, maintain, and control space (whatever we call it - virtual, nonplace, network) links us to notions of power and necessarily to issues of authority, dominance, submission, rebellion, and cooperation". Thus, we feel a need for systems that teachers and researchers can use to better understand the effect of their behavior in this complex environment. We next describe each of the three categories of teaching presence, as well as indicators that are later used to measure the extent to which each category of teaching presence is represented in the transcript of a given online course.

Design and Organization

As in many forms of distance education, the process of designing and planning the online course is usually more extensive and time-consuming than is the analogous process in classroom based teaching. More thorough planning often results when teachers work on courses that may be visible to peers, administrators and visitors as well as their own students. Building the course in a digital format forces teachers to think through the process, structure, evaluation and interaction components of the course. Much of the learned expectation of classroom norms is not available for either student or teacher use, and thus the teacher is forced to be more explicit and transparent in their planning process. We refer to this component of teacher presence as design and organization.

Activities in this category of teaching presence include building curriculum materials including the creation and integration of external 'learning objects' such as those available through MERLOT. 'Re-purposing' materials, such as lecture notes to provide online teacher commentaries, mini-lectures, personal insights and other customized views of course content, is another common activity that we assign to this category of teaching presence. This category also involves designing and administering an appropriate mix of group and individual activities that take place during the course. This category of teaching presence also includes the processes through which the instructor negotiates time lines for group activities and student project work, a very important aspect of online courses.

Many researchers have documented the challenge to the instructor of synchronizing activities so that learners feel "in synch" with the rest of the class. The teacher also provides organizational service to students by providing guidelines and tips and modeling appropriate etiquette and effective use of the medium. This includes appropriate use of the reply and quote functions, and repair of communications breakdowns such as inappropriate posting or postings placed in the wrong discussion forum.

Students also need to have a sense of the "grand design" of the course and reassurance that participating in the learning activities will lead to attainment of their learning goals. We concur with Laurillard, Stratfold, Lukin, Plowman and Taylor that the teacher's task is to create a narrative path through the mediated instruction and activity set such that students are aware of the explicit and implicit learning goals and activities in which they participate. Macro-level comments about course process and content are thus an important motivation and orientation component of this category of teaching presence.

Facilitating Discourse

Facilitating discourse during the course is critical to maintaining the interest, motivation and engagement of students in active learning. We use the term discourse rather than discussion to highlight the focused and sustained deliberation that marks learning in a community of inquiry or as Scardamalia and Bereiter refer to it, the " knowledge-building community." In fulfillment of this component of teaching presence, the teacher regularly reads and comments on student postings, constantly searching for ways to support the development of the learning community.

This component overlaps with many of the behaviors identified in our larger model of "social presence" as the teacher is an active member of the community of inquiry. However, the teacher's role is more demanding than that of other participants, and carries with it higher levels of responsibility for establishing and maintaining the discourse that creates and sustains social presence.

The teacher shares responsibility with each individual student for attainment of agreed upon learning objectives. The teacher supports and encourages participation by modeling appropriate behaviors, commenting upon and encouraging student responses, drawing in the less active participations, and curtailing the effusive comments of those who tend to dominate the virtual space. Unlike the analogous categories used by previous researchers, our facilitating discourse category is more than the facilitation of social activities. Our facilitating discourse function differs from the "social dimension" of computer conferencing, which Henri defines as "statements not related to formal content or subject matter". Rather, facilitation of discourse is usually integrated within direct instruction and in situ design of instructional activity. Under this heading we place teacher postings that stimulate social process with a direct goal of stimulating individual and group learning. Therefore, we tend not to search in the "coffee room" or "chat" areas of the computer conference for evidence of these indicators, but do look for indicators of support for social discourse within each message in the content focused discussions. Their presence indicates the teacher is helping to create a positive learning environment.

The indicators we use to identify the facilitating discourse component of teaching presence include the identification of areas of agreement and disagreement. From a Piagetian perspective, cognitive development requires that individuals encounter others who contradict their own intuitively derived ideas and notions and thereby create cognitive conflicts. It is the resolution of these conflicts that results in higher forms of reasoning. Teachers may be required to help students find congruent linkages when two seemingly contrary opinions are being expressed.

Similarly, helping students articulate consensus and shared understanding, when these are already implicit in the discussion, is also useful. Finally, the teacher's facilitation tasks include assessing the efficacy of the process. Computer conferencing has become associated with large time commitments from teachers and students. Thus, we look for indicators that the teacher is "moving the discussion along" and insuring effective and efficient use of time.

Direct Instruction

In this final teaching presence category, teachers provide intellectual and scholarly leadership and share their subject matter knowledge with students. Davie writes that the instructor must be able to set and communicate the intellectual climate of the course or seminar, and model the qualities of a scholar. The students and the teacher have expectations of the teacher communicating content knowledge that is enhanced by the teacher's personal interest, excitement and in-depth understanding of the content.

The cognitive apprenticeship model espoused by Collins & Brown, Rogoff's model of apprenticeship in thinking or Vygotsky's scaffolding analogies illustrate an assistive role for teachers in providing instructional support to students from their position of greater content knowledge. Although many authors recommend a "guide on the side" approach to moderating student discussions, this type of laissez faire approach misinterprets a fundamental element of peer collaboration models. A key feature of such social cognition models is the adult, the expert or the more skilled peer who scaffolds a novice's learning. The role of the teacher, in any context, involves direct instruction that makes use of the subject matter and pedagogical expertise of the teacher.

Some theorists have argued that online teaching is unlike classroom based teaching in that the "the teacher must adopt the role of facilitator not content provider" . The arbitrary distinction between facilitator and content provider we find troublesome. Garrison in a lively exchange focused on differentiating so called teacher-centered and student-centered instruction, makes the point that "the self-directed assumption of andragogy suggests a high degree of independence that is often inappropriate from a support perspective and which also ignores issues of what is worthwhile or what qualifies as an educational experience".

The role of "e-moderator" which likens the teacher to a facilitator of learning. Her description suggests that the e-moderator does not require extensive subject matter expertise. She writes, "they need a qualification at least at the same level and in the same topic as the course for which they are moderating". We believe that such minimal subject level competency provides less than the ideal that defines high quality professional education. We recognize that economic factors and intense demand for instruction in some content areas may result in large scale educational programs being designed around "big distance education" models that, through specialization and skill differential, provide adequate learning experiences for some subjects.

However, we believe that there are many fields of knowledge, as well as attitudes and skills, that are best learned in forms of higher education that require the active participation of a subject matter expert in the critical discourse. This subject matter expert is expected to provide direct instruction by interjecting comments, referring students to information resources, and organizing activities that allow the students to construct the content in their own minds and personal contexts. Presentation of content and directing questions to the group or to individual students is an important, traditional role for the teacher. Teachers also provide focus to the discussion by directing attention to particular concepts or information that is necessary to frame or pursue knowledge growth.

A widely documented problem in computer conferencing is the difficulty of focusing and refining discussions so that conversation progresses beyond information sharing to knowledge construction and especially application and integration. We believe that this stalling of the discussion at the lower levels of the critical inquiry process occurs when there is not adequate teaching presence in the computer conference. The teacher's summary is also normally not merely a neutral "weaving" of the previous postings. It often serves to develop and explicitly delineate the context in which knowledge growth has taken place. Direct instruction also takes the form of statements that confirm understanding through assessment and explanatory feedback.

Assessing student comments is time consuming and requires higher levels of knowledge than that commonly held by student participants. Often a small component of the formal course assessment relates to student participation in the conference, but in addition informal and timely teacher assessment and feedback is especially useful and valued by students. Diagnosing misconceptions is another critical task of the on-line teacher. Often students hold misconceptions that impair their capacity to build more correct conceptions and mental schemata.

The design of effective learning activities leads to opportunities for students themselves to uncover these misconceptions, but the teacher's comments and questions as direct instruction are also invaluable. The teacher is also familiar with a wealth of resources to which they can refer students for further individual or group study. The number, quality and accessibility of these resources are increasing exponentially as more information is digitized and made available via the World Wide Web. Finally, the teacher may be asked to provide direct instruction on technical questions related to access to the conferencing system, manipulation of the conferencing software, operation of other tools or resources, and the technical aspects of dealing with any of the subject related tools and techniques.

The descriptions of three categories of teaching presence in the previous section provide a starting point for assessing and investigating the corresponding roles that are filled primarily by the online instructor, though often with the aid of other individuals such as instructional designers. In this section, we present a method of assembling empirical evidence in support of the existence of teaching presence and its three categories by analyzing the transcripts of computer conferences that form part of graduate level university courses. The method utilizes a research technique called content analysis, defined as "a research methodology that uses a set of procedures to make valid inferences from text".

The set of procedures includes identifying and defining a target variable, collecting samples of representative text, and devising reliable and valid rules for categorizing segments of the text. Ultimately, this process culminates in descriptive or inferential conclusions about the target variable. A definition of our target variable, teaching presence, and a description of its three categories has been provided above. To facilitate the classification of transcript segments into the categories, we have listed the pedagogic roles subsumed under each category and provided examples of how these roles are typically performed in conferences. The process of selecting segments of a transcript requires the researcher to stipulate what the segments or units of analysis will be. Rourke et al. identified five units of analysis that have been used in computer conferencing research including proposition units, sentence units, paragraph units, thematic units, and message units. Of these five, they determined that thematic units were by far the most commonly used by researchers, although message units were the most practical.

Thematic units are identified based on their correspondence to a particular category definition. The thematic unit allows coders to capture variables in their natural form; however, it is a prohibitively labor intensive process. It is also difficult to maintain what Hagelin calls unit reliability, defined as "the consistency in identifying what is to be classified, i.e., the amount of information to be included in each unit." Using the message as the unit of analysis, coders generally assign an entire message to one category. The use of message units is less time-consuming and facilitates unit reliability; however, this unit has been characterized as alternately too large or too small to adequately characterize a single item of data.

We again used the message unit. However, rather than simply assigning each message unit that demonstrated some sort of teaching presence to one and only one of the categories of teaching presence, we allowed for the possibility that a single message might exhibit characteristics of more than one category. Therefore, each message posted by the instructor was coded as exhibiting or not exhibiting one or more indicator of each of the three categories of teaching presence. This procedure proved to have a number of advantages for our investigation. First, the number of coding decisions was pre-determined for the coders - three decisions per message. This was useful for alerting coders to the need to make a decision and provided a denominator for calculating reliability.

Second, the system was quickly implemented and did not require coders to determine the number or the exact text length of indicators present per unit of analysis. Third, totals for each category are easily determined and meaningfully expressed by reporting the percentage of total teacher postings that contains each of the categories. We feel that procedure is reliable, efficient, and practical. Ultimately, the validity of this system will be judged according to two criteria: Does the procedure facilitate the objective quantification of the insights that an observer would gain from an informal reading of the transcripts? And does the procedure reveal additional insights that are not apparent from an informal reading?

In order to establish the reliability of the coding procedure, two raters were assigned to code all messages in both of the 13-week conference transcripts. As a result of using the message as the unit of analysis, unit reliability was 100%. Interrater reliability, defined as "agreement among coders about the categorization of content," was determined using Cohen's kappa. Cohen's kappa is a chance-corrected measure of interrater reliability that assumes two raters, n cases, and m mutually exclusive and exhaustive nominal categories. The formula for calculating kappa is:

$$k = (F_o - F_c) / (N - F_c)$$

Where:

N = the total number of judgments made by each coder

F_o = the number of judgments on which the coders agree

F_c = the number of judgments for which agreement is expected by chance.

Interrater reliability for the distance education transcript was k = .77; for the Health Promotions transcript, interrater reliability was k = .84. Riffe et al. report "research usually reports reliability figures in the .80 to .90 range. Research that is breaking new ground with concepts that are rich in analytical value may go forward with reliability levels that are somewhat below that range."

Table 2 shows the frequency and percentage of teaching presence categories that were observed in the messages posted by the instructors of two graduate level, distance education courses. Percentages were calculated by dividing the total number of postings showing a given category of teaching presence by the total number of messages posted by that instructor. Direct instruction was the predominant category, with between 77% and 88% of all teacher messages including some form of direct instruction. Instructional design was the least frequently observed category of teaching presence, with between 22% and 38% of messages addressing instructional design.

Table 2

Frequencies of teaching presence categories by instructor

	Health Course		*Education Course*	
	f	%	*f*	%
Instructional Design	31	22.3	12	37.5
Facilitating Discourse	60	43.2	24	75.0
Direct Instruction	107	77.0	28	87.5

Table 3 illustrates the frequency and percentage of instructor messages that addressed 0, 1, 2, or 3 of the categories of teaching presence. 64% of the Health Promotions instructor's messages included only one category of teaching presence. For the Distance Education instructor, the largest percentage of messages included two categories of teaching presence.

Table 3

Frequency and percentage of messages that included 0, 1, 2, or 3 categories of teaching presence

	Graduate Health Course		*Graduate Course*	*Education*
	f	%	*f*	%
0 categories	1	0.7	0	0.0
1 category	89	64.0	7	21.9
2 categories	42	30.2	15	46.9
3 categories	7	5.0	10	31.3

Our results show the pattern of teaching presence varying considerably between these two courses facilitated by two experienced online teachers. The education teacher made use of student moderators during the later weeks of the course, and thus the number of teacher postings were considerably reduced compared to the health teacher who responded to almost every student posting. In the education course, the student moderators were performing a substantial part of the teaching presence role. We have observed this phenomenon in a number of online courses. This supports our decision to refer to this element of the community of inquiry as "teaching presence" rather than "teacher presence," as a number of individuals who are not teachers often collaborate in carrying out this role. Again with regard to the two courses we examined, it should be noted that the education instructor made far fewer postings, but those postings covered, on average, a considerably higher number of the categories of teaching presence, as compared to the more frequent postings of the health sciences instructor.

Among teachers of online courses, generally, there are probably many individual variables that affect the number and content of the instructors' postings and hence their contribution to teaching presence in the conference. These will include teaching style, discipline related conceptions of the education process, size of the class, and the teachers' and students' familiarity and expertise with the medium. We report above only the aggregate totals of each of our three categories of teaching presence. It may be useful to use frequencies of individual indicators in further studies that focus on one of the three major functions of the CMC teacher that we have identified.

The tool may also be used as a diagnostic instrument for teachers to analyze and compare the magnitude and pattern of their "teaching presence" with that of other teachers. Finally, we can see applications in which hypothesis testing is done related to any number of determinants of teaching presence, including work load, subject matter expertise, nature of the learning activities, and the teacher's previous experience in conventional or technology enhanced instruction.

Activities in, particularly, the instructional design category of teaching presence start well before the actual course starts, but unlike 'canned forms' of distance education, online teaching allows the instructor to revise and augment content and learning activities as the course progresses. As much of the work of this phase precedes the establishment of computer conferencing based interactions, many of the roles of this category are not visible to the students or researchers in the computer conference transcript. Thus, the record we examine is only a subset of this activity. Further, some of the teacher presence activities do not take place in common forums and are conducted through private email, voicemail or telephone. Thus, the conferencing transcript provides a snapshot and an indicator of teacher presence activities. These organizational functions vary considerably based on the features and services of the 'system' within which the formal courses are offered. The usefulness of this tool relates to its simplicity and its diagnosis capacity. Coding using our format is relatively easy and training procedures necessary to achieve reasonably reliable results are not as time consuming as other schemes we have used.

More importantly we see practicing teachers as well as researchers being able to review their postings and look for or note the absence of each of the three indicators of teaching presence. Thus, the system can be used to diagnose teaching difficulties, to help teachers reduce workloads by increasing the quality and reducing the quantity of their messages, and to increase the semantic density and functionality of their postings. The tool may also be used to analyze and describe differences in style between different types of teachers, teachers of different disciplines or to assess the contribution of student moderators or others assigned to perform ancillary teaching functions.

Marshall McLuhan is famous for his insight that "the medium is the message," implying that the impact of the medium is integral to and in some cases determinant of the message. Certainly teaching in an online environment is influenced by the absence of the non-verbal communication that occurs in the face-to-face settings of conventional education, and the reduction in the amount of paralinguistic information transmitted, as compared to some other modes of distance education such as video or audio teleconferencing. However, McLuhan also noted that each new medium takes a preceding medium for its content, and that the process of interpreting a new medium in terms of an older one (horseless carriage effect) filters our conception of the newer medium. This process of viewing the new medium through the conceptual filter developed for the older medium necessarily colors our understanding of the teaching process in a computer mediated communications (CMC) context. Part of the challenge, as mentioned above, is to develop compensatory behaviors for the relative lack of non-verbal and paralinguistic communication in a text-based medium such as computer conferencing.

Another part of the challenge is to overcome the difficulty of conceiving the role of the teacher in online courses within the long established conceptual framework that we have built in the context of conventional, face-to-face teaching. Feenberg suggests that this is problematic because teachers have difficulty transposing leadership skills developed in the rich medium to the leaner medium of the text-based conference. We are not convinced that the function of teaching changes, though certainly its manifestation looks quite different in this mediated context. Especially in these "pioneering days" of online learning the thoughtful design of learning activities is critical to the attainment of educational outcomes. In the process of designing and using these tools, teachers are forced to be learners themselves and like all who experience learning, the learners themselves are changed.

The conceptual framework to understand, measure and improve the important function of "teaching presence" within a computer conference environment. We invite others to use and refine the concept and the tools piloted in our study, in order to better provide theoretical and empirical information to help the many pioneer online teachers of this decade.

6

Enhancing Students' Creativity and Thinking Skills

Computer Literacy

As computers become more widely used in schools, educators have invented many different ways to use them. The different uses for computers are based on quite diverse models of what the purposes of computer education should be. One very common approach is based on the notion of "computer literacy": the idea that there is some basic familiarity with computers which *all* students need in order to compete in the job market, or to be informed citizens.

Several educators have questioned the specific details of particular "literacy" plans, while accepting the overall concept. "Computer literacy doesn't mean X," they say, "it means Y." For example, Arthur Luehrmann says, "[C]omputer literacy must also mean the ability to *do* computing, and not merely to recognize, identify, or be aware of alleged facts about computing." His argument is that a computer curriculum should give students actual programming experience, not just reading about computers in a book. But Luehrmann accepts the concept of computer literacy itself, the idea that there is *something* which every student must learn. He questions only the details of just what this something is.

What we would like to do is call into question the claim that there is anything about computers which belongs in the school experience of *every* student. We agree with Luehrmann that programming can be a valuable experience. But the word "literacy" means more than that; it means that everyone must have the experience in order to be able to function at all in society.

The word "literacy" is a magic word, which conjures up a very strong metaphor. Literacy in its original sense, knowing how to read, really *is* universally required in our society. Any educator who suggested eliminating reading from the curriculum would be laughed at, if not tarred and feathered. Merely to say the phrase "computer literacy" definitively answers a question which has not explicitly been asked. It's like the classic "When did you stop beating your wife," but harder to recognize because it is so widely used.

One practical result of the literacy metaphor is that many decisions about computer education have been made in a kind of panic. Parents call up the school committee to ask why their children are not being trained for the vital computer job skill. These parents may not know just what that skill is, and neither does the school committee. But they do know that the private school down the road has computers.

It's quite true that more and more jobs involve the use of computers. That's different from saying that these jobs involve computer *expertise*. Let's look at some examples. A good example of a computer-using job is that of selling hamburgers at McDonald's. That machine behind the counter which looks like a cash register is actually a computer terminal. When you order a Quarter-pounder with cheese, instead of ringing up whatever the price is, the counter person pushes a button which says "Quarter-pounder with cheese." The computer displays the price, but it also keeps track of how many of this item are sitting under the heat lamps. If they're running short, the computer tells the cooks in the back to make more. The same computer can tell the manager to buy more hamburger buns at the right time. It's a pretty sophisticated system, and helps make McDonald's a low-overhead operation.

Now, what does the person behind the McDonald's counter need to know about computers? He only needs to know that when you ask for a Quarter-pounder with cheese, he should push the button which says "Quarter-pounder with cheese." That's it. Nothing about input unit, output unit, processor, and memory; nothing about programming either.

Perhaps a more common example is that of computer word processing. The word processor involves a much more intimate interaction with the computer than selling hamburgers. Still, the manufacturers of word processing systems take pains to *hide* the computer, to make the way you operate the machine as much as possible like operating an ordinary typewriter. What skills does a word processing operator need? For the most part, exactly the same skills a secretary needed before word processing: good spelling and punctuation, touch typing, being able to read the boss's handwriting. What the computer adds is mostly a matter of pushing the "paragraph" button instead of the carriage return and the tab.

There are more specifically computer-related skills, of course, like threading the fanfold paper into the printer. But that's the sort of thing which is done differently for each specific model, and which is part of a very specific job training program. It isn't what you'd teach in a "computer literacy" course for everyone.

Perhaps the point really is that there are too many *different* computer-related skills to teach all of them to every student. Using a spreadsheet program, for example, is very different from using a word processor. Using a microprocessor-controlled automobile engine tester is very different from either. Neither "this is the return key" nor actual programming will help much with any of those job activities.

The notion of computer literacy grew up in the first place as an accident of history, because of the great speed with which computers have become important. Curriculum developers are, by and large, 30 or 40 or 50 years old. They grew up in a world without computers. Suddenly, they have had to face up to a shocking change in the very nature of the world around them. In inventing computer literacy courses, they have designed a curriculum *for themselves*, not for the kids who have grown up with Pacman, automated bank tellers, and bar code readers in the supermarket.

Another, more sophisticated reason is a confusion about the role of education in social mobility. Many people think that by learning to program computers one can get a good job. The problem with this idea is that what works for a few people stops working when everyone does it. Many years ago, hardly anyone had a high school diploma. Those who did have one could get the cream of the jobs. A few decades ago, about half the population of the United States graduated from high school. They didn't get the very best jobs—by then, you needed a *college* diploma for that—but they did get decent and fairly secure jobs. Now, almost everyone has a high school diploma, and it's worthless.

Similarly, the day of the matchbook-cover computer school as the route to riches is already over. There are many openings for computer programmers, but the jobs go to people with Computer Science doctorates, preferably with experience. There is still room for the programming entrepreneur, but the people who succeed in that role are not the product of computer literacy courses. They are computer enthusiasts who do it *because it's fun*, not because it's homework.

The effect of the "computer literacy" movement will be the opposite of what is intended. In the early days, when very few schools offered such courses, their alumni really did have a competitive edge in the job market. But as we approach the day when every school offers "literacy" courses, a day eagerly sought by those who believe in the literacy metaphor, there will be more "literates" than jobs. Those who have taken the courses won't find easy jobs. But those who *haven't* taken the courses will be completely out of luck. Ironically, the literacy metaphor will become self-fulfilling, not because there is any real need for such training, but because employers will start demanding it as a filter for job applicants, just as there is no *real* basis for requiring a high school diploma for many jobs today.

The computer can be an appealing medium for learning for some students, without being forced upon every student. Computers are a general-purpose tool; they may appeal to different students in different ways. One student may like graphics and animation. Another may like electronic mail. Another may prefer video games. The architecture and scheduling of a computer facility should encourage all these diverse uses.

Another right idea is to make the computer available to students as a serious tool, in their lives *right now*, not as something they'll need later. Probably the most important example of this approach is word processing. Students have to write many papers, for English teachers, history teachers, and so on. Word processing can make the mechanics of this task much easier, encouraging second drafts. Instead of setting up a required course, try just letting students know that this facility is available to them if they want it. But provide enough printers to handle the load!

For students who are interested, the computer can be valuable not as narrow job training, but as a medium for developing problem-solving skills. It can also be a medium for developing independence, since not every student need be doing the same programming project at the same time. This educational use of computer *programming* is the central idea behind the Logo approach to computer education.

Teaching Basics of Computer Hardware

A computer is a programmable machine (or more precisely, a programmable sequential state machine). There are two basic kinds of computers: analog and digital.

Analog computers are analog devices. That is, they have continuous states rather than discrete numbered states. An analog computer can represent fractional or irrational values exactly, with no round-off. Analog computers are almost never used outside of experimental settings.

A digital computer is a programmable clocked sequential state machine. A digital computer uses discrete states. A binary digital computer uses two discrete states, such as positive/negative, high/low, on/off, used to represent the binary digits zero and one.

Computers are used for a wide variety of purposes.

— *Data processing* is commercial and financial work. This includes such things as billing, shipping and receiving, inventory control, and similar business related functions, as well as the "electronic office".

— *Scientific processing* is using a computer to support science. This can be as simple as gathering and analyzing raw data and as complex as modelling natural phenomenon (weather and climate models, thermodynamics, nuclear engineering, etc.).

— *Multimedia* includes content creation (composing music, performing music, recording music, editing film and video, special effects, animation, illustration, laying out print materials, etc.) and multimedia playback (games, DVDs, instructional materials, etc.).

Parts of a Computer

The classic crude oversimplication of a computer is that it contains three elements: processor unit, memory, and I/O (input/output). The borders between those three terms are highly ambigious, non-contiguous, and erratically shifting.

A slightly less crude oversimplification divides a computer into five elements: arithmetic and logic subsystem, control subsystem, main storage, input subsystem, and output subsystem.

— processor

— arithmetic and logic

— control

— main storage

— external storage

— input/output overview

— input

— output

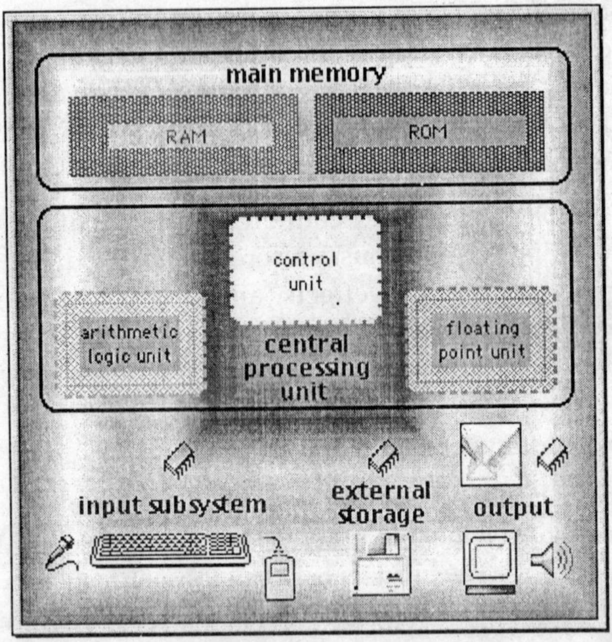

Figure 1. Parts of a Computer

Processor

The processor is the part of the computer that actually does the computations. This is sometimes called an MPU (for main processor unit) or CPU (for central processing unit or central processor unit).

A processor typically contains an arithmetic/logic unit (ALU), control unit (including processor flags, flag register, or status register), internal buses, and sometimes special function units (the most common special function unit being a floating point unit for floating point arithmetic).

Some computers have more than one processor. This is called multi-processing.

The major kinds of digital processors are: CISC, RISC, DSP, and hybrid.

— *CISC* stands for Complex Instruction Set Computer. Mainframe computers and minicomputers were CISC processors, with manufacturers competing to offer the most useful instruction sets. Many of the first two generations of microprocessors were also CISC.

— *RISC* stands for Reduced Instruction Set Computer. RISC came about as a result of academic research that showed that a small well designed instruction set running compiled programs at high speed could perform more computing work than a CISC running the same programs (although very expensive hand optimized assembly language favored CISC).

— *DSP* stands for Digital Signal Processing. DSP is used primarily in dedicated devices, such as MODEMs, digital cameras, graphics cards, and other specialty devices.

— *Hybrid* processors combine elements of two or three of the major classes of processors.

Arithmetic and logic

An arithmetic/logic unit (ALU) performs integer arithmetic and logic operations. It also performs shift and rotate operations and other specialized operations. Usually floating point arithmetic is performed by a dedicated floating point unit (FPU), which may be implemented as a co-processor.

An arithmetic/logic unit (ALU) performs integer arithmetic and logic operations. It also performs shift and rotate operations and other specialized operations. Usually floating point arithmetic is performed by a dedicated floating point unit (FPU), which may be implemented as a co-processor.

Control

Control units are in charge of the computer. Control units fetch and decode machine instructions. Control units may also control some external devices.

A bus is a set (group) of parallel lines that information (data, addresses, instructions, and other information) travels on inside a computer. Information travels on buses as a series of electrical pulses, each pulse representing a one bit or a zero bit (there are trinary, or three-state, buses, but they are rare). An internal bus is a bus inside the processor, moving data, addresses, instructions, and other information between registers and other internal components or units. An external bus is a bus outside of the processor (but inside the computer), moving data, addresses, and other information between major components (including cards) inside the computer. Some common kinds of buses are the system bus, a data bus, an address bus, a cache bus, a memory bus, and an I/O bus.

Main storage

Main storage is also called memory or internal memory (to distinguish from external memory, such as hard drives).

RAM is Random Access Memory, and is the basic kind of internal memory. RAM is called "random access" because the processor or computer can access *any* location in memory (as contrasted with sequential access devices, which must be accessed in order). RAM has been made from reed relays, transistors, integrated circuits, magnetic core, or anything that can hold and store binary values (one/zero, plus/minus, open/close, positive/negative, high/low, etc.). Most modern RAM is made from integrated circuits. At one time the most common kind of memory in mainframes was magnetic core, so many older programmers will refer to main memory as core memory even when the RAM is made from more modern technology.

Static RAM is called static because it will continue to hold and store information even when power is removed. Magnetic core and reed relays are examples of static memory. Dynamic RAM is called dynamic because it loses all data when power is removed. Transistors and integrated circuits are examples of dynamic memory. It is possible to have battery back up for devices that are normally dynamic to turn them into static memory.

ROM is Read Only Memory (it is also random access, but only for reads). ROM is typically used to store thigns that will never change for the life of the computer, such as low level portions of an operating system. Some processors (or variations within processor families) might have RAM and/or ROM built into the same chip as the processor (normally used for processors used in standalone devices, such as arcade video games, ATMs, microwave ovens, car ignition systems, etc.).

EPROM is Erasable Programmable Read Only Memory, a special kind of ROM that can be erased and reprogrammed with specialized equipment (but not by the processor it is connected to). EPROMs allow makers of industrial devices (and other similar equipment) to have the benefits of ROM, yet also allow for updating or upgrading the software without having to buy new ROM and throw out the old (the EPROMs are collected, erased and rewritten centrally, then placed back into the machines).

Registers and flags are a special kind of memory that exists inside a processor. Typically a processor will have several internal registers that are much faster than main memory. These registers usually have specialized capabilities for arithmetic, logic, and other operations. Registers are usually fairly small (8, 16, 32, or 64 bits for integer data, address, and control registers; 32, 64, 96, or 128 bits for floating point registers). Some processors separate integer data and address registers, while other processors have general purpose registers that can be used for both data and address purposes.

A processor will typically have one to 32 data or general purpose registers (processors with separate data and address registers typically split the register set in half). Many processors have special floating point registers (and some processors have general purpose registers that can be used for either integer or floating point arithmetic). Flags are single bit memory used for testing, comparison, and conditional operations (especially conditional branching).

External storage

External storage (also called auxillary storage) is any storage other than main memory. In modern times this is mostly hard drives and removeable media (such as floppy disks, Zip disks, optical media, etc.). With the advent of USB and FireWire hard drives, the line between permanent hard drives and removeable media is blurred. Other kinds of external storage include tape drives, drum drives, paper tape, and punched cards. Random access or indexed access devices (such as hard drives, removeable media, and drum drives) provide an extension of memory (although usually accessed through logical file systems). Sequential access devices (such as tape drives, paper tape punch/readers, or dumb terminals) provide for off-line storage of large amounts of information (or back ups of data) and are often called I/O devices (for input/output).

Input/output Overview

Most external devices are capable of both input and output (I/O). Some devices are inherently input-only (also called read-only) or inherently output-only (also called write-only). Regardless of whether a device is I/O, read-only, or write-only, external devices can be classified as block or character devices.

— A character device is one that inputs or outputs data in a stream of characters, bytes, or bits. Character devices can further be classified as serial or parallel. Examples of character devices include printers, keyboards, and mice.

— A serial device streams data as a series of bits, moving data one bit at a time. Examples of serial devices include printers and MODEMs.

— A parallel device streams data in a small group of bits simultaneously. Usually the group is a single eight-bit byte (or possibly seven or nine bits, with the possibility of various control or parity bits included in the data stream). Each group usually corresponds to a single character of data. Rarely there will be a larger group of bits (word, longword, doubleword, etc.). The most common parallel device is a printer (although most modern printers have both a serial and a parallel connection, allowing greater connection flexibility).

— A block device moves large blocks of data at once. This may be physically implemented as a serial or parallel stream of data, but the entire block gets transferred as single packet of data. Most block devices are random access (that is, information can be read or written from blocks anywhere on the device). Examples of random access block devices include hard disks, floppy disks, and drum drives. Examples of sequential access block devcies include magnetic tape drives and high speed paper tape readers.

Onput

Input devices are devices that bring information into a computer.

Pure input devices include such things as punched card readers, paper tape readers, keyboards, mice, drawing tablets, touchpads, trackballs, and game controllers.

Devices that have an input component include magnetic tape drives, touchscreens, and dumb terminals.

Output

Output devices are devices that bring information out of a computer.

Pure output devices include such things as card punches, paper tape punches, LED displays (for light emitting diodes), monitors, printers, and pen plotters.

Devices that have an output component include magnetic tape drives, combination paper tape reader/ punches, teletypes, and dumb terminals.

Generally speaking, teaching and learning activities in the CELT general-education (GNED) courses were structured within the so-called "arts and technology domains". We structured the course with "arts" contents while encouraging the use of "multimedia technology" as a means for students' to express their ideas in digital format. These two elements were involved in different courses to differing extents. Within this context, teaching and learning activities engages students in an active-learning environment that consists of various hands-on activities requiring students to explore and experience different ways of expression.

While the arts and the use of multimedia technology served as the foundation for course planning, an "artistic process" served as the central principle for this active learning approach to be applied to all of these courses at various levels. In general, students participated in creative activities and technical skill workshops in multimedia disciplines, which aimed to provide students with a stimulating learning environment to experience the 'artistic process'. This process required students to act as:

- artists/creators - working actively in creating their works
- performers (or presenters) - aiming to enhance students' presenting and communication skills
- audiences - learning to appreciate
- critics - learning to think critically

The above four roles are inter-related and are expected to help in realizing the "active learning" process among students as students are more likely to "internalize, understand, and remember material learning through active engagement in the learning process".

GNED002 The Creative Process

This course aims to develop students' artistic thinking through experience in art activities. Besides attending lectures on art and cultural issues in the context of Hong Kong, students were required to select one kind of art-form workshop from drama, music composition with MIDI, creative video, and dance. These workshops involved students actively in brainstorming, organizing, analyzing, synthesizing, evaluating, improvising, and performing or presenting ideas. The final project lays emphasis on students going through the so-called "creative processes". Usually students will form into groups to work out their "mixed-media" work. This project requires students to express an original idea through drama, music, video work, or movement/gesture. This is also a valuable opportunity to collaborate, research a topic, evaluating each other's ideas, and synthesize ideas with students who come from different kinds of workshop, and to strike for a common goal-the final product, which has to be presented or performed using any kind of media (or combination thereof).

GNED003 Arts and Technology

In this course, "active learning" occurs when students appreciate, think about, and create art works. Artworks in various disciplines, including visual, music, installation and multimedia elements, were introduced to enable students to develop their aesthetic sense, cultural awareness, and global outlook. Aesthetic value in arts is emphasized here and students will go through more in-depth, high-order thinking processes in due course.

In order to enhance students' critical thinking abilities, we emphasized in-depth discussion among students focusing on art and cultural issues and their relationship with technological development. This was carried out during tutorials and on-line discussion forum using the "computer support intentional learning environment" (Scardamalia, M, Bereiter, C, Mclean, R S, Swallow, J & Woodruff, E, 1989). Strategies of using this tool will be discussed in details in the following section.

Creating a piece of artwork is a must for a student going through the so-called "artistic process". Before they accomplish their work in digital form or present their work by multimedia means, students have to research their chosen theme/topic. This serves as the foundation on which they build their work.

GNED004 Multimedia Communication Skills for Internet Applications

In this course, the use of "technology" was encouraged as a means of communication and expression. Students in lectures went through basic communication theories with illustrations from daily-life examples. However, this only served the purpose of "knowing the knowledge", and students did not necessarily receive what they are expected to learn. Therefore, project-based assignments were introduced for them to demonstrate how they apply the knowledge acquired. Using multimedia means, such as in graphics, text, sound, or video footage formats, etc., students were required to accomplish projects relating to storytelling, self-portrait, and promoting ideas on the Web. Students' ideas had to be presented through digital media such as video, web pages, and/or a combination of them. These projects are designed to convey messages to the audience persuasively and convincingly. A brief research report was required from each group of students relating to the project content.

"Computer-supported Intentional Learning Environment"

As one of the objectives of GNED courses is to develop students' critical-thinking skills, a "computer-supported intentional learning environment"-Knowledge Forum® 3-was adopted in GNED002 and 003 to facilitate the online discussion process among students during art appreciation activities and critiques. Students had to work out their conclusion in response to a topic or problem. According to the rationale, students have to "build" their knowledge by collaborative exploration of the issue, while collaboration is realized through a computer network that enables students to work whenever and wherever possible.

As in the example here, a topic was set out for students to discuss: "Is art important to our society?" Knowledge Forum® 3 (KF3) provided the discussion space in which all communication data were stored in a database. Students who engaged in the discussion could log into the database whenever they wanted and contribute their notes in response to the topic. This environment enabled them to develop their argument by "building-on" others' ideas (by specifying their ideas according to preset "scaffolds" for cognitive operation) that can be shown visually on screen.

Discussion notes archived inside KF in GNED003 showed that students were thinking actively and openly within this collaborative learning environment. Students reflected frequently on their own and others' ideas and also built on others' ideas. The situation is in fact a "growing process" from a preliminary idea, query, or problem. Its effects on students' development of aesthetic values, and critical-thinking abilities as well as metacognitive ability, are far reaching.

Feedback from Students on the Instructional Approach

Evaluation data were collected from three sources: questionnaire surveys, students' discussion notes from the KF3 database, and interviews with students and instructors. The evaluation instruments were specially designed to examine students' changes in attitudes and values, as well as their self-perception in relation to concepts of arts and creativity.

Content analysis of students' discussion notes form KF database

In the case of GNED003 and GNED002, students' discussion notes were examined in detail and focused on exploring the following aspects:

— The number of keywords students used in discussion

— The frequency of appearance of the keywords

— The number of times the individual student quoted the keywords

— The number of times each student commented on other's ideas

— Students' idea flow - Have students changed their discussion focus during the course?

— Whether students have modified their preliminary arguments
— The number of "build-on" ideas of each student
— The frequency of each student quoting others' ideas
— The comparison of students' final argument with their original argument
— Whether students have worked out "their" conclusion in response to the topic/problem
— Individual student's degree of participation

Interviews with Students and Instructors

Interviews with randomly selected students helped us gain an in-depth understanding of their feelings about and comments on the courses. Information from this source was valuable as it reflected students' experiences from a "target audience" point of view. Moreover, interviews with instructors helped our understanding of the problems arising from course planning and coordination.

Lessons Learned and Looking Ahead

From the curriculum design process and the reflections by students and instructors, the active-learning approach seems to be effective and successfully implemented. Several implications can be drawn at this stage:

— a free and relaxed environment is essential for students to develop creative thinking. From observing and reviewing students' works, we can see that students very much enjoyed the creative process. Students' comments from interviews revealed this obviously.
— Learning effectiveness seemed to be at its highest point when students engaged in the active-learning process.

Hands-on activities in workshops, discussion among students and collaborative work, seemed to help students to apply the knowledge they acquired in their work, as well as developing their higher-order thinking skills. Experiencing the so-called "artistic process" is a good means of developing their creative, aesthetic, and presentation and communication skills.

— It is the responsibility of the instructors to help students to realize that technology is a means rather than an end in their work. Students often produce fancy subject matter without rich or meaningful content by using multimedia technology. Multimedia technology can be an effective means of expression, but students should bear in mind that it is just a means of expressing their ideas.

— As reflected from the statistical results of students' feedback, there is still room for improvement in motivating students to work collaboratively. Moreover, the exposure time in specific art forms was not adequate enough for them to understand and experience the subject matter. Therefore, it is essential to make use of the opportunity to merge students from different art disciplines to work together. This might provide them with the opportunity to cooperate, share, and express themselves in alternative ways.

— students indicated that they sometimes get lost during the course, and also that the lecture content was sometimes too abstract for them to relate to their work. Therefore, it is necessary to have better planning and structure of the lecture content so as to strengthen their understanding of what we expect students do in their assignments.

- Strategies for evaluating students' works are essential for establishing an objective assessment system. Rubrics for assessing students' work may help students to achieve meaningful and effective compositional process.

General-education courses in higher education can be an excellent means for students to develop their creative and critical-thinking skills. For such courses to be effective, the instructors must provide students with sufficient space, guidance, stimulus, and encouragement so that they will be willing to try out their ideas and be able to learn through self-exploration and peer interaction. Active learning is thus an important instructional strategy that can serve as the fundamental principle in planning these courses. However, the current evaluation strategies are not perfect enough to reflect the effectiveness of the instructional approach, since performance and thinking in arts are difficult to measure. More research in this aspect is needed in contributing to future development along these lines.

7

Interactive Education Technologies

A quantitative synthesis of studies of the effectiveness of interactive distance education using videoconferencing and telecommunications for K-12 academic achievement. Effect sizes for 19 experimental and quasi-experimental studies including 929 student participants were analysed across sample characteristics, study methods, learning environment, learner attributes, and technological characteristics. The overall mean effect size was 0.147, a small positive effect in favour of distance education. Effect sizes were more positive for interactive distance education programmes that combine an individualized approach with traditional classroom instruction.

Programs including instruction delivered through telecommunications, enhancement of classroom learning, short duration, and small groups yielded larger effect sizes than programs using videoconferencing, primary instruction through distance, long duration, and large groups. Studies of distance education for all academic content areas except foreign language resulted in positive effect sizes. This synthesis supports the use of interactive distance education to complement, enhance, and expand education options because distance education can be expected to result in achievement at least comparable to traditional instruction in most academic circumstances. Between 1989 and 1996, the number of instructional computers in schools increased over 200% and by 1997, the number of schools with Internet access had reached 70%.

In today's education climate, use of current technology becomes increasingly critical in schools for several reasons. Schools that are able to demonstrate innovative educational strategies using technology are at a distinct advantage in attracting and keeping top students, and in earning further funding through grants, endowments, and programs. Of course, having technology does not ensure effective use of the tools, and therefore may not translate into education benefits. Schools are pressured by their communities to show that the investment is paying dividends in educational achievement. Educational administrators and decision-makers are challenged with providing increased educational opportunities without increased budgets.

Many educators are responding to this challenge by developing distance learning projects. As of 1995, 60% of all personal computers in K-12 schools were networked to another computer. Half of all school districts were using distance learning in the business of education: academic modules and credit courses, driven by demand for time and place independence and by economic issues. Eighty two percent of the states reported that equality of educational experience in all schools was the principle need addressed by distance education projects that provided courses to homebound and remotely located learners. Distance learning applied physical technology and education processes to serve the needs of students when they are removed from the source of instruction and resources by either time or distance. As with most instructional tools, the purpose of distance learning is to help schools meet the instructional needs of their students and to enable students to access information more effectively and apply what they learn in school to the world in which they live.

Distance learning uses a group of systems to bring teaching and learning together by transmitting information or expertise from one place to another for the benefit of the learner. Formally, distance education is characterized by physical separation of learners from the information, an organized instructional program, use of technological media, and two-way communication. The benefits of distance education as outlined by Kerka include flexibility to meet specific needs, providing equity of educational opportunity to students in varying localities, low-cost alternatives, new learning experiences, and expanded resources.

Organizational learning forms infrastructures to enhance and extend the capabilities of the individual to collaborate and to use specialized knowledge of others. All forms of education are enhanced by the increased access to information and communication afforded through distance education. Disadvantages of distance education include sound and video that may be less than broadcast quality, reliance on learner initiative to work in a situation with less supervision than a classroom, the need for technical skills to work with the delivery technology, and the possibility of social isolation.

Distance acquisition of knowledge is often an expensive and time-consuming process to institute and maintain. It is important to know whether it actually improves student performance. It is also critically important to know which distance education delivery methods and techniques are more effective, so students get maximum benefit from society's investment in distance learning technology. Faced with so many new, rapidly changing options, schools need data in order to make quality decisions regarding distance education. A review of distance education literature reveals well-developed theory supported by extensive experimental study.

However, distance education research has not been subjected to repeated review and synthesis, especially in regards to K-12 education. Holmberg's theory of distance teaching states that distance teaching will support student motivation and promote learning pleasure and effectiveness if learners are engaged in discussions and decisions, and the program provides for real and simulated communication to and from the learners. As in any classroom, interaction is the core of teaching.

Distance education is believed to work very well, and produce results as effective as traditional classroom instruction . However, the distance education currently in practice has the potential to provide more effective learning with updated pedagogy, more experience, and greater understanding and knowledge of methods. Numerous studies have evaluated student achievement in specific distance learning programs in higher education. According to Abrami and Buras , learning at a distance is seldom superior to traditional instruction, particularly for promoting higher level achievement and complex skills. These weaknesses may stem from social and intellectual isolation. Improved distance education practices have the potential to enhance educational outcomes, especially when the amount and kind of learner interaction is increase using technology-supported collaborative learning. Although distance learning is well documented with adults, fewer studies of effectiveness exist that center on the primary and secondary levels. At a point when all states offered distance education in schools, very few had conducted formal evaluations. While it is possible that our knowledge of distance education technology in higher education is relevant with precollege learners, there is no empirical evidence for this assertion.

Additionally, previous research has spread across grade levels, content areas, and technologies. Distance education program developers have paid less attention to the appropriate blend of media, content, learner, and gain; instead defining effectiveness in terms of the number of students served or student satisfaction.

Purpose of the Meta-analyses

In light of the lack of previous meta-analyses on the issue, the purpose of the current study was to arrive at a comprehensive assessment of the effectiveness of interactive distance education for K-12 learners. This meta-analysis had two main goals. The first goal was to determine the effects on K-12 student achievement of interactive distance education use of video-conferencing or online telecommunications. Traditional reviews of distance education literature conducted in the 1980's indicate that learners achieve as well in distance education programs as they do in traditional classroom settings.

Other studies described by Moore and Thompson indicate that the instructional format itself has little effect on student achievement as long as the delivery technology is appropriate for the content, and timely teacher-to-student feedback is included. This research involved technology that is now outdated, and was not conducted using quantitative synthesis methods. Good distance teaching practices have been found to be fundamentally identical to good traditional teaching practices, with quality factors being universal across environments and populations.

This means not only that various studies of distance learning may be synthesized reliably, but also that the results of such a synthesis ought to generalize to most comparable education situations. Meta-analyses have been performed recently to show trends correlating use of technology in general with improved achievement , but not focused on distance education. The second main goal of this study was to identify the features (duration of use, frequency of use, instructional design, delivery system, ability of students, level of students, content area) of the most effective interactive distance education systems.

The Software Publishers Association reported evidence that educational technology's positive effects depend on subject area, student population, and level of access to technology. The present quantitative synthesis of studies was an effort to increase understanding of the effectiveness of distance learning on K-12 achievement by revealing the features and combinations of characteristics that make distance education most effective.

Studies involving student academic achievement as a result of distance education at the K-12 level were assembled. Quasi-experimental studies were included with experimental studies because true experiments are done in artificial situations, while quasi-experiments usually occur in more realistic conditions. Quasi-experiments, although having lower internal validity, produce more realistic results and increased external validity. The setting for the studies was K-12 learning environments, with preference for studies using random sampling. Both published and unpublished studies were included to avoid publishing bias.

Studies were gathered from computer databases including ERIC, Dissertation Abstracts, requests from national and state distance education projects, and the World Wide Web (WWW or Web). Searches were systematically conducted in journals of education organizations from the 1980s and 1990s because of the recent development of the distance education delivery systems being examined there. Searches employed the keywords distance education, distance learning, teleconferencing, videoconferencing, satellite, telecommunications, and email.

The technology directors for each state were contacted by email with requests for data. These initial searches unveiled references for hundreds of documents. Each document was located in ERIC files, on the Web, in journals, by interlibrary loan, or by ordering dissertations. After examination, studies were included in the meta-analysis when they met all inclusion criteria:

(a) a focus on the use of interactive distance education technology for education at K-12 levels, either videoconferencing or online telecommunications;

(b) publication between 1980 and 1998;

(c) experimental or quasi-experimental design providing quantitative outcomes from which effect size can be estimated; and

(d) freedom from obvious flaws.

The bibliographies of studies that did not meet all inclusion criteria provided references for locating other studies. When studies lacked data for inclusion in this analysis, a direct request was made to the authors or sponsoring organization to send additional information. A total of

59 such requests were sent by way of post or e-mail. A preliminary group of 59 studies was selected from all available studies for review to determine their appropriateness for inclusion in the meta-analysis. Of the 59 studies reviewed, 40 were eliminated for reasons including insufficient data on student achievement, failure to focus exclusively on K-12 learners, focus on attitude rather than achievement.

Coding and Interrater Agreement

Studies included in the meta-analysis were reviewed and coded independently by two doctoral students. The general categories of coding were publication characteristics, technological characteristics, ecological characteristics, methodological characteristics, and analytical results. Interrater agreement for all studies averaged 85%, and exceeded 80% for all categories of coding. In cases where agreement fell below 80%, the study was examined and the coding process was clarified. Percent agreement was calculated for each study by dividing the number of agreements by the total number of features coded, then multiplying by 100.

Classification of Variables

The dependent variable in this synthesis was student achievement in the academic content area measured by instruments appropriate to the individual study. The measure of student performance in the studies was indicated on achievement measures given at the end of the distance education period. Such measures included standardized tests and teacher/researcher designed instruments. Traditional measures may not be effective in assessing the effectiveness of distance education systems that strengthen higher order skills.

Complex skills such as problem solving, motivation, writing, collaboration, and awareness of community are some of the benefits of using distance education. Growth in these areas can only be inferred with the use of common achievement measures. The student performance measures used in the studies analyzed here are accepted as the best estimates of the effect of interactive distance education technology on student achievement currently available.

Dependent measures were coded into one of eight content areas, one of three types of achievement measure, and one of four testing sequences. The content areas were general, language arts, mathematics, science, social studies, computer science, and foreign language. The types of achievement measures were standardized, teacher-developed, researcher-developed, and other. The testing sequences were pretest-post-test or posttest only. The treatment variables related to interactive distance education were categorized by duration, frequency, instructional design, and delivery system.

Student characteristics including ability level and grade in school were also coded. Comparisons were made between distance education programs in which students used the technology for less than a half-year of instruction and those in which the technology was used for at least a half year. Programs exposing students to distance education activities almost daily were contrasted with programs in which students participated in distance education on a weekly basis. Within instructional design, studies were coded as either using distance education as the primary instructional delivery system, or as using distance education systems to supplement regular classroom instruction.

The distance education delivery system was e-mail, Web, or two-way audio-video conferencing. Student groups were coded on the grade level designations primary, intermediate, middle, or high school, and were classified as functioning at regular ability levels or advanced.

Effect Size Calculation

The achievement data reported in each study contributed to the calculation of effect size for the meta-analysis. Cohen's effect size is a standardized estimate of the difference in achievement between students learning with interactive distance education and students learning with traditional methods. Effect sizes were computed as the difference between the control and experimental posttest mean scores divided by the average standard deviation. For studies in which a group of students was evaluated using multiple achievement measures, effect sizes were found for each measure, and then averaged.

The average effect size was used in the overall effect size estimate of the meta-analysis. For studies in which more than one independent group of students was evaluated, an independent effect size was found for each group and used in the meta-analysis separately. While different groups tested in one study were dependent with respect to study features and characteristics, the samples were independent. A correction factor based on Hedges, Shymansky, and Woodworth was applied to each biased effect size to remove bias by accounting for sample size. The independent effect sizes were combined by weighted averaging to yield an overall effect size estimate. Heterogeneity of effect sizes was estimated to determine the appropriateness of combining them into an average. A formal analysis of heterogeneity (ANOVA) was completed for the effect sizes with effect size as the dependent variable, and the study features as factors. The *p*-value for the ANOVA was also set at 0.01. This procedure enabled conclusions to be drawn regarding the significance of levels of variables. For example, the ANOVA may reveal that a certain level or type of learner achieves at significantly higher levels using a specific distance education system.

In addition to the overall student performance, effect sizes were reported for each variable. Effect size comparisons were made with respect to the following variables: duration frequency, instructional design, delivery system, ability level, grade level, and content area. Effect sizes were also compared for the study characteristics date of study, source of study, hardware components, achievement measure, and sample size.

The 19 independent effect sizes calculated in this synthesis compared students learning with interactive distance education technology with students learning with traditional classroom instruction only. The weighted mean effect size across all studies was 0.147 (SD = .69). The mean sample size for the studies was 48.9 (SD = 13.2). The mean grade level of the students was 8.3, with a standard deviation of 0.59. The average study measured student achievement after 14.7 weeks of distance education (SD = 2.6). Studies using two-way audio-videoconferencing as the distance education system comprised 68% of the total, followed by 26% of studies that used e-mail, and one study using the Web. The most common academic content area for the studies was science, approximately 32% of the studies. All other content areas made up less than 16% each. All studies took place in school classroom environments. All studies except two involved regular level learners, and the remaining two studied advanced learners.

The average year of publication for the studies was 1993 (SD = .71), with dates ranging from 1986 to 1997. The most frequent source of studies was dissertations (68%), followed by journals, and the World Wide Web. Approximately 84% of authors were affiliated with universities. In terms of the experimental design, two-thirds of the studies used a quasi-experimental design, and one-third were experimental. Only 10% of the studies made use of random assignment to groups, while 53% used convenience groups such as school classes.

The remaining studies grouped students based on other criteria such as volunteering or parent selection. A full 74% of studies employed a pretest-posttest design, and 36% used posttest only. The most common form of measurement instrument in the studies was researcher-developed tests (32%), followed by teacher-developed and standardized (26% each), and publisher-developed tests (16%).

Distance Learning Environments

For analysis, the effect sizes were classified into 12 categories related to features of the studies. Effect sizes above Cohen's threshold for marginal, magnitude (below 0.45) occurred for studies of telecommunication, weekly use of distance education, use of distance education to supplement class-room instruction, mathematics and other subject areas (computer science and general elementary), and intermediate grade levels. Effect sizes above Cohen's 0.80 cutoff of 'large' effect size were found only for the other subjects, and for foreign language in a negative direction. Seven studies in this synthesis had heterogeneity values above 5.3, indicating that they were 'strikingly deviant' To further investigate the significant heterogeneity, analysis of variance of effect sizes was used.

The heterogeneity in the studies is unexplained. The optimal method for combining effect size estimates with unexplained heterogeneity is the random effects model. Random effects procedures treat between-study variations in effect sizes as random. The procedures begin with the estimation of between-study variance, used to determine the difference between the observed variance among effect sizes and the with-in-study sampling variance.

The sample variance for the 19 studies in the meta-analysis is 0.481. The between-study variance was found to be 0.413. This variance was used in calculating confidence limits and in combining the effect size estimates in the random effects model. The effect size formula was weighted with both the within-study sampling error variance (standard error) and the variance. The overall effect size for the 19 studies is 0.147, considered a small positive result. The standard error of the effects weighted average is 0.159. This result is a small positive effect size. At an alpha level of 0.05, the 95% confidence limits were constructed by multiplying the square root of the variance, 0.413, by 1.96, then adding and subtracting from the effect size, d+. In this case, the confidence limits were -1.113 and 1.407. Because the interval encompasses zero, the null hypothesis that the population effect size is zero cannot be rejected. Interactive distance learning techniques cannot be considered to be more or less effective than traditional instruction.

Because of the near-significant result of the ANOVA for subject area and the cluster of outliers, a second overall effect size was estimated without the foreign language studies. The random effects, effect size estimate for the meta-analysis was 0.344, discounting foreign language studies. The affect size improves after accounting for these discrepant studies in post hoc analysis, although the confidence interval of -0.686 to 1.374 still encompasses zero. The overall standard deviation for the random effects effect size estimate was found. The result for the 19 studies is a standard deviation for effect size of 0.480.

The meta-analysis presented here examined a sample of studies that met established inclusion criteria, including data from 929 learners. The analysis encompassed a broad view of K-12 interactive distance education by focusing on the range of subject areas, grade levels, and applications of distance education in use today. The questions of the overall effect on K-12 academic achievement of interactive distance education, and of the features of effective distance education systems were addressed through the use of random effects effect size estimation and analysis of variance. The study design permitted review of a wide sample of research done on academic achievement of students learning with distance education. The overall effect size for interactive distance education on K-12 learning was the small positive 0.147, accounting for sampling error and variance. The 95% confidence interval for the random effects weighted effect size was -1.113 to 1.407. In comparing levels of the variables delivery system, grade level, ability level, content area, instructional design, duration, and frequency of use, and the study features of date, source of study, achievement measure, testing sequence, and sample size, no significant differences were found. In a post hoc analysis after eliminating the outlier foreign language studies, an effect size of 0.344 was calculated, with a confidence interval of -0.686 to 1.374. As a result of the statistical processes applied in the meta-analysis, the overall effectiveness of interactive distance education has been estimated as it is used for K-12 learning. Interactive distance education was found to have an average effect size of 0.147, translating to a gain of 0.147 standard deviations on average for a student at the 50th percentile learning with distance education over traditional methods.

No significant differences were detected between grade levels, subject areas, ability levels, distance education technology, duration and frequency of use of distance education, or instructional design in relation to learning. However, the three foreign language studies made a close approach to significance with strong negative effect sizes. Consequently, distance education can be expected to result in achievement at least comparable to traditional instruction in most academic circumstances. Educators planning implementations of distance education programmes should expect no difference in academic performance as a result of the use of distance education. More importantly, when implemented with the same care as effective face-to-face instruction, distance education programmes can be used to complement, enhance, and expand education options for students, at least at intermediate, middle, and upper grades levels.

Implications

In a time when standards-based education has taken on a greater real-world, situated focus, it has become more important for educators to provide students with authentic connections to a learning environment beyond the school boundaries. Interactive distance education is a vehicle for extending the reach of student influence into the community, as well as a means of including the family and community in a learning conversation. In light of the findings of this meta-analysis, supplementing traditional instruction with distance education can enable more reality-based learning, with possible achievement gains.

The benefits of such educational enhancement in terms of attitude and interpersonal workplace skills are unknown at the present time. Under pressure to present learners with greater opportunities at lower cost, educational leaders may find that offering courses to secondary learners through interactive distance education effectively enlarges the course catalogue and students worldview at the same time. On a cautionary note, distance education for K-12 is much newer and less proven than traditional instruction.

The fact that only 19 studies were found to be suitable for this analysis is a testimony to that fact. Therefore, students and teachers have fewer quality materials and less experience on which to draw when using distance education. It can be argued that as the use of interactive distance education grows and expertise develops, academic gains can be expected to increase. In the area of foreign language instruction, great potential exists theoretically for linking students with native speakers and writers, but the results of the studies reviewed here indicate that distance education in foreign language should be studied closely. The three foreign language studies in this meta-analysis reported that students learning with distance education systems performed demonstrably lower than students learning in traditional classrooms. While foreign language options are needed in high schools, distance education courses for foreign language instruction should be evaluated very carefully.

8

Online Course Design and Delivery

In recent years there has been a tendency for instructors at all levels to put their teaching materials on the Internet, either for distance-learning or ease-of-access purposes. Designing instructional materials for online teaching and learning is quite a challenge to instructors in any field. Teaching materials of this kind can be quite different to those used in traditional classrooms or lecture theatres, in the sense that they must somehow replace or compensate the role or presence of the instructor.

Other items traditionally found in classrooms or lecture theatres, e.g., hard-copy handouts, demonstrations and even Q&A, must also be substituted or compensated accordingly. In the early days, prior to WebCT or other similar packages, one might have to rely solely on custom-built HTML templates for laying out teaching materials in Web language. Fortunately these days are over. Nowadays, there are more than a handful of well-designed Web-course packages available for instructors to transform their teaching materials for Web-viewing without first acquiring a detailed knowledge of Web-programming. The article is divided into two parts. The aim of the article is to discuss the methodologies used and report the difficulties encountered during the course design.

Teaching Materials Design for Online Learning

Building materials for online learning is a challenge because they differ markedly from their counterparts in the traditional classroom; they have to take the role of the teachers, or more accurately, compensate for the absence of teachers. Traditionally, the handouts distributed to students during the class may not be self-contained. This need not or should not be so, since the lecture itself will fill the gaps in the handouts.

The gap may exist because the teachers want the students to think, to understand more, or, at least, to concentrate. Surely there should be textbooks or references for students to read after the class. If online teaching materials are like the traditional handouts, the online students would still need go to the classroom; otherwise they are worse off. Online learning has to do more to help our students. Online teaching materials have to be redesigned. Without the presence of the teachers, what should they look like? How can they motivate students to read them, to understand them, and to think deeper? Would adding multimedia components help? Or should we consider instructional design too? Should we sit back and think again if we were to expect the same result from classroom teaching?

MS Power Point as Notes for PHYS007

Initially the Power Point (PPT) version of the notes was developed to serve two purposes: To allow the developer to become familiar with the ideas in the notes; and to make the lecture more lively and help the instructor to explain the ideas. They are put on the course web as a supplementary component of the course, together with the HTML and PDF version of the notes. The HTML and PDF notes consist mainly of text. Since Spring 2000, when PHYS007 was first offered, the PPTs are found to be very useful according the reactions of students and other audiences. They generally think that the PPTs are attractive and can help a lot in explaining complicated physical ideas. We realize that PPTs can be an important component for online learning where the teacher is not always there to stimulate students.

This is a comment from the developer of PPTs:

> "When making the Power Points, it was as though I was making "graphical" notes while following ideas from the text. This actually makes the flow smoother in making and the resulting Power Points are quite self-explanatory. They can serve as self-study materials besides being used in class presentations!"

When asked which kinds of notes are most useful to them, students' responses are diverse. PPT can get the students' attention and lead the flow of thought. It emphasizes important points more than plain text does. It is good for ordinary students. On the other hand, for bright students who are eager to learn or for those who already have pictures in their mind, they feel that the flying graphics in the PPT are annoying. They prefer plain text in PDF or HTML. HTML is very flexible, though it demands more technically capable developers. It can theoretically embed any object in it. One can insert multimedia and other interactive components into the notes. However, the size of each page matters. Waiting for objects to show up in the page turns students down. PPT, on the contrary, can be downloaded as a whole to the students' side and be read off-line, thus performance is guaranteed. We believe that before fine-tuned HTML notes are fully developed, we should put up all note formats. PPT can act as a virtual teacher to stimulate the students when the real teacher is not there. The plain text versions are the textbooks used for deeper thinking. PPT has the further advantage that it is light, easily available, and flexible. It technically requires less from the developer and hardware. It is easy to learn, and it is likely that the developer is already familiar with it. It is available on nearly every machine in the world. Teachers can edit the content any time, anywhere. Updates can be made easily. We note that using PPTs to explain physics is non-trivial. It is an art that requires good physical pictures and good visual design from the developers. Such a process requires digestion and organization of ideas, which are far from mechanical.

WebCT and other Multimedia Components

Before we start discussing our use of WebCT for delivering the course PHYS007, let us recap a little what WebCT really is. WebCT is short for Web Course Tools, developed by a team in the Department of Computer Science at the University of British Columbia, headed by Murray Goldberg. The software package was first released in May 1996 and it is now being used by more than 900 universities around the world. Although it looks and feels like a Web page and is even viewed using a Web browser, it is not a Web page. WebCT consists of an integrated set of components for developing, delivering and managing interactive Web courses over the Internet. It has a wide variety of interactive and communication components integrated both in function and appearance. Having everything under one platform greatly simplifies course development and management. The main features of WebCT are student ID management, multiple forums, and chat rooms, calendar with timed announcements, self-testing, quizzes, student progress, glossary, and so on.

The main reason for choosing WebCT as a platform for online delivery of our course PHYS007 was a result of intensive discussion with the Center for Enhanced Learning and Teaching (CELT) at HKUST. After deliberating and comparing all the advantages and disadvantages in terms of functionalities and ease-of-use with other platforms/ packages currently available, we have eventually concluded that WebCT is the best available platform for delivering our PHYS007 course. The first thing we must do in designing an online course such as PHYS007 is to repackage everything in an online format. For PHYS007, the complete set of teaching materials includes lecture notes, quizzes, assignments, and projects.

In the traditional PHYS007, all these components are available simply as PPT and PDF printouts. In order to convert these components suitable for online delivery, we have to take into account several constraining factors such as availability of computer software and network bandwidth. In determining which computer software to use, we also take into account which software is less likely to cause a computer crash during network delivery. The advantage of using RealMedia for video and audio streaming is its capability to encode the original file into a relatively smaller file with only a slight drop in quality. With its small file size and superior network protocol, the lecture notes with added voice-commentary could be viewed even with a normal 56k modem at home. This is actually quite important because it enables those who don't have broadband access at home to view the lecture notes in their own time. Apart from the voice commentary, some video teaching materials were also encoded in RealMedia format for online delivery. Other items such as demonstrations, quizzes, assignments, and Q&A have all been transformed online.

The demonstrations are video-recorded and then encoded in RealMedia format for online delivery. The quizzes are reprogrammed in WebCT native language and delivered at a pre-specified time using WebCT's built-in time function. The assignments are simply relocated into the WebCT platform and delivered as normal assignments with added time control. Finally, the live Q&A is replaced by online Q&A with live video assisted by chat-room-style keyboard communication. The advantages and limitations of using a variety of multimedia are variable. WebCT does not yet have the video and audio streaming functions built into the package. At the moment, there is simply no single package that can cover everything required for designing and delivering an online course with course management tools. We just have to ask ourselves what we want to deliver, what's needed, and what's available. At least that seems to be the best solution for now.

Experience tells us that it is hard to stimulate students to read online materials. For a course requiring Active Learning like PHYS007, the problem cannot be simply solved by setting examinations or otherwise forcing students once more into drill and practice patterns. Therefore, a better instructional design should be considered. We find that explaining concepts in physics without face-to-face contact is difficult. At this stage we solve the problem by arranging classroom tutorials. Online learning will probably have more impact on the style of instruction than wiping out large numbers of classroom offerings in a single swoop. Surely classes can be made shorter and many people will be able to learn with fewer class visits needed. Although we expect that online courses will save resources in the long run, instructional and teaching materials development of a working online course is highly time and resources consuming. Course suppliers and fund providers should understand that technology just solves the easiest part of the problem in online learning. At the time of writing, there is simply no single package that can cover everything required for designing and delivering an online course with course management tools.

WRITING AND SPEAKING THROUGH THE CURRICULUM PROGRAM (WSC)

The "Writing and Speaking through the Curriculum Program" (WSC) began as a "pilot project" in the spring semester of 2000 in USA. Initially, the HKUST School of Business and Management (SBM) wanted to emphasize the importance of English language skills among its undergraduate students through a "content-based approach". The obvious benefits of a similar approach were also noted by Martha Iancu in 1997 at George Fox University in Oregon, USA. Similar to the situation in Hong Kong, it was noted that students were highly motivated to succeed, particularly in credit-bearing academic courses.

Extra ESL courses, therefore, helped them to develop essential language skills necessary for their university studies. Teachers also found the academic content and language linked approach useful: "Collaboration with other faculty members has enhanced mutual understanding, appreciation, and respect for the activity of preparing non-native English speakers for U.S. college courses". It should be noted, however, that in the U.S. case study, ESL adjunct courses were offered to ESL students based on academic subject areas. This is rather different from the WSC program. At HKUST, the WSC program assessment tutors assess the first draft of a content-based assignment for language. The second draft is subsequently assessed by subject faculty for content. The fact that English language skills are crucial to both the academic and future career success of students has also proven to be a point of "common ground" for academic faculty and English language teachers at HKUST. As a result, a growing mutual understanding of how subject content and English language skills are inextricably woven together is raising the awareness of all concerned. It is from this common awareness, therefore, that SBM originally requested the assistance as well as expertise from the Language Center (LC). Although the WSC is a jointly coordinated program, it is administered and managed by the LC, with assistance provided by SBM in terms of faculty and student participation.

Under the management of the Language Center, the primary objective of the work carried out by the WSC team is to help undergraduate SBM students to further enhance their English language communication skills by working directly with their subject professors. In an effort to achieve this broad objective, therefore, WSC staff work with faculty from all six departments of the School of Business and Management on a single content-based short written assignment. On average, the WSC team works with approximately 20 subject professors and their students, and they assess between 1,500 and 2,000 written assignments per semester. Although the assignments are confined in length to one to two pages only, the sheer amount of text being dealt with is, to say the least, substantial. In addition to assessing the written assignments, the WSC Assessment Tutors (AT) meet with students on an individual basis in an effort to provide extra assistance with the preparation of final drafts of assignments. Students are able to book 20-minute individual appointments with an AT any time through the WSC website.

The WSC Assessment Procedure

The WSC team itself, is a unique group comprised of both experienced language teachers as well as business professionals from such places as Canada, the United States, India, the UK, and Hong Kong. Drawing upon the expertise of each individual member, the team serves as a rich resource for HKUST undergraduate students of SBM. They work closely with professors who are participating in the program in order to assist them with the setting, coordination, and assessment of their short course-related written assignment. Following the setting of the assignment, the Assessment Tutors offer advice on how to manage the task, as well as communicate the requirements to the students through pre- and post-class visits.

Students submit the first draft of their designated course assignment to their assigned Assessment Tutors. This assignment is subsequently assessed for language. Feedback is provided for students on a cover sheet using a standard list of common errors. The feedback typically consists of comments on grammar, sentence-level language errors, logic, and coherence. Suggestions for further improvement and a reference materials checklist are also provided.

The first drafts are then returned to the students so that they can absorb the written feedback that is provided and, if necessary, they can make an individual consultation appointment with their Assessment Tutors for a more in-depth discussion about their writing. After revising their work, students then prepare another draft. This final draft is then submitted to their professors for content grading.

WSC Workshops and Mini-courses

The Assessment Tutors are also involved in the development and teaching of workshops and mini-courses for groups of SBM students who are interested in signing up on a voluntary basis. The workshops and mini-courses are specifically targeted at language skills that students need in both the academic as well as business environments. Teaching materials, video productions, role-play scenarios and even interviews with business people are all part of the workshop and mini-course teaching materials. Topics that have been developed include: The Language and Structure of Business Cases, Speaking Skills in the Business Context, Proposal Writing, and Language Skills for Business Meetings.

Evaluation Procedures

The WSC Program is evaluated at the end of each semester by both students as well as faculty participants. Questionnaires are sent out via e-mail, and participants are asked to comment on their experience of engaging in the WSC. They are also asked for comments and suggestions that may be considered for future improvements to the program. In addition to this, WSC assessment tutors are also asked to offer their views with regard to the program at the end of each semester. This information is collected, analyzed and, if feasible, implemented as the program develops.

As a university funded initiative, the WSC Program was recognized as an example of "Good Practice in Teaching and Learning" by the Senate Committee on Teaching and Learning Quality in May 2001. The committee noted in particular that the program "weaves the learning of language and communication skills into the study of the curriculum... and it demonstrates a new team approach that cuts across disciplinary and organizational boundaries, pooling expertise from different disciplines." To date, the WSC Program has been running for four semesters. Although it was initially launched as a "pilot scheme" in

January 2000, it has been improved considerably with the addition of a WSC website, a larger number of trained assessment tutors from both education and business backgrounds, and generally more support from SBM faculty and students. Perhaps a worthy note of conclusion is the fact that studies have shown that approximately 75% of a managers' daily work is spent communicating in either the written or spoken forms.

9

Teacher Professional Engagement

Teachers vary in how they conceptualize their role—their duties and responsibilities as teachers. Some teachers view their work as taking place solely within their classrooms in what is essentially a private, individual practice. They are content to let educational decisions about curriculum, policies or standards be made by outside experts, and they accept that different teachers choose to teach in ways that they themselves believe are ineffective or wrong. Instead, they focus on trying to be the best teacher they can be with the students in their own classroom. Others view their responsibilities as extending beyond classroom teaching to include participation in the larger community of educators and administrators. They see their role as trying to help other teachers be more successful and to influence how teaching occurs in other places. Although few teachers see teaching exclusively in one way or the other, it may be useful to think of this contrast as a continuum from private to professional practice. How teachers define their role will determine how they spend their limited time both in and beyond the classroom.

Traditionally, the job of teaching involved accepting sole responsibility for the education of a small group of students over some period of time, often working alone. As schools grew in size, the organization shifted to graded classrooms for younger students and subject-specific courses for older students, and to having more teachers and students in the same school building. But the structure of one teacher to each class of 15 to 35 students has remained remarkably uniform. Many teachers use their autonomy to implement their personal theories about teaching and learning in their subject-area, while others use the closed door to hide their difficult struggle with the complexity of teaching. For the latter group, to ask for or offer help risks assumptions of incompetence or interference with the autonomy of others.

Teachers with a private orientation have little time for meetings, conferences, or other forms of professional engagement. Teachers employ the textbooks and other teaching resources which they are given or which they gather themselves, and orchestrate their own instructional practices without significant input from others. They may do this because of perceived disagreements between their own perspective and those of their peers or because of a sense that the norms of their craft do not permit admitting that one needs help from peers in order to do one's work. In either case, their choice is to engage in a private practice.

Professional Practice

A contrasting orientation to teaching sees it as a collective endeavor rather than a private practice of individual teachers. Teachers today are expected to prepare all students to reach significantly higher academic standards than have ever been attempted in this country. In this situation, an individual teacher can never know enough to warrant closing the classroom door. Collegiality is the logical inverse of privacy and personal control.

We refer to the opposite pole of a teacher's role orientation, not as "collaborative" but as "professional." Teachers with a professional work orientation not only try to help other teachers do a better job in their classrooms, but they also see their responsibility in terms of the larger community of educational practitioners. Their concern about what happens in other classrooms becomes part of their own definition of being successful. For example, when teachers with a professional work-orientation experience pressure from school, district, or state recommendations that contradict their studied beliefs about good teaching, they work collectively to formulate a collective but substantive response rather than expecting each teacher to resolve the conflict individually. Teachers who adopt a collaborative stance toward teaching are more likely to build a professional identity than those engaged in private practice. This professional identity includes publishing papers, offering workshops and speaking at conferences. They view their relationship to other educators within and beyond the school as an important determinant of the quality of student learning in the classroom.

These two contrasting orientations will affect the way that teachers interact with their colleagues. In this study, we look at the nature of teacher interactions with other teachers at the same school, with teachers at other locations, and with the larger educational community–particularly interactions that suggest professional leadership in that community. We will use these markers to identify teachers who view teaching in professional terms and contrast such teachers with those whose lack of interactions with other teachers suggest a more private practice. We then examine how the presence or absence of social relationships within and beyond the school affect teachers' own classroom teaching and, in particular, their use of computers.

Our data on teachers' role orientation, beliefs about teaching, and teaching practices comes from a national survey, conducted during the Spring of 1998, that focused on the relationship between teacher pedagogy and their use of computers in teaching. The study was funded by the National Science Foundation with additional funds provided by the Office of Educational Research and Improvement, U.S. Department of Education. Called Teaching, Learning, and Computing–1998 (TLC), the survey involved questionnaire responses from three different samples of schools–a national probability sample of schools (655 participated of 898 sampled); a purposively drawn sample of schools with the greatest per-capita computer technology (110 schools participated), and a purposively drawn sample of schools that were participating in some way in substantial educational reform efforts, either self-initiated or as part of one of 50 different national or regional reform programs (450 schools). Within each school, the TLC survey collected data from the principal, the school technology coordinator, and a probability sample of teachers. The teachers were selected in a way that disproportionately over-sampled those who made substantial use of computers, who had students do project work, and who emphasized higher-order thinking in their teaching. However, all analyses use weights that compensate for differential sampling rates of different types of teachers so that the results can be seen as coming from a representative sample of teachers at the schools surveyed.

The teachers whose responses are described in this report number 4,083, including 2,251 in the national probability sample of schools. The teachers are those who taught classrooms from the 4th through the 12th grades in all subjects except physical education and special education. The teachers completed 20-page survey instruments. Some survey questions were asked to subsets of respondents (four different overlapping questionnaire versions were used), so some of the data was not based on the full sample surveyed. The teacher respondents are 69% of the teachers originally sampled; and the schools participating include 75% of the schools initially selected.

The four-category measure, level of Professional Engagement, used in this report is based on teachers' responses to three multi-part survey questions. The first question dealt with two kinds of within-schoolinformal interactions a teacher might have–discussions with other teachers about teaching issues; and their experience in observing other teachers' classroom instruction as well as being observed by these same teacher-peers. The second question dealt with beyond-school contacts–sustained professional contact with teachers at other schools through committee work, multiple conference attendance, and electronic mail. The third question concerned the teacher's recent involvement in specific leadership activities–mentoring other teachers, presenting at workshops, teaching at universities, and publishing. For each of the three survey questions, criteria were defined to indicate "high" and "medium" levels of engagement in that particular area. Teachers who scored "high" in all three areas (within-school, beyond-school, and leadership) we designated as "Teacher Leaders." Those who had scores of at least "medium" in each area we designated "Teacher Professionals." The remaining teachers were designated either "Interactive Teachers" or "Private Practice Teachers" based on their combined score on the three survey-question-based indices. In the following section, we discuss teachers' responses to each of the three multi-part survey questions, and then show the kinds of responses that placed teachers into one or another level of Professional Engagement.

Within-School Interaction

A teacher's Within-School Interaction was defined as the average frequency that the teacher reported having each of six types of interactions with other teachers at their own school. Those interactions included discussions about teaching methods, project ideas, subject-matter issues, technology, and informal observations of another's or one's own teaching.

For each one of the four types of informal discussions that we asked about, about one-third of all teachers reported having at least weekly discussions, and 10% reported having daily interactions around these topics. For example, 12% of teachers said they had discussions with other teachers about ideas for student or group projects "almost daily," while another 23% said they had those kinds of discussions "1 to 3 times per week."The same teachers who discussed one of the four topics also tended to discuss the others. Thus, while one out of six teachers (16%) said that they had informal discussions at least weekly about three or even all four topics, a substantial minority of teachers (43%) indicated that they didn't have weekly conversations about any of them. In contrast to the reasonably common practice of holding informal discussions on substantive topics, only a small minority of teachers regularly observe one another's teaching. Slightly more than one teacher in five (21%) reported observing other teachers at least "several times per month" and a similar number reported being observed that often themselves. Observations occurring as often as weekly was reported by very few teachers (4 to 5 percent).

We combined teachers' responses to the "informal discussion" interactions and the "classroom observation" interactions (each with responses coded 1 to 4) to compute an average measure of Within-School Interaction. A teacher whose six types of informal interactions averaged halfway between "several per month" and "one to three times per week" was classed as "high" in Within-School Interaction, and this designation was one of the three standards for being defined as a Teacher Leader. A "medium" score, leading to the designation of being a Teacher Professional, was based on an average answer of "several per month." Overall, 13% of 4th through 12th grade teachers in the probability sample met the "high Within-School Interaction" criterion and 27% other teachers met the less rigorous "medium" criterion. However, because teachers who collaborate within their school don't necessarily collaborate beyond their school and don't necessarily engage in leadership activities, only a small minority (16%) of teachers who met the "high" criterion for Within-School Interaction also met parallel standards on the other two aspects of teacher professional engagement and thus became classified as Teacher Leaders. Similarly, only about one-fourth of those who met the less rigorous "medium" standard in terms of their Within-School Interactions also met at least a medium standard in both of the other two aspects of professional engagement.

Beyond-School Contact

The second question used to define levels of Professional Engagement asked teachers about their interactions with teachers at schools other than their own. "Beyond-School Contact" was defined in terms of three types of cross-school contacts that teachers might have: attending workshops, participating on committees, and emailing teachers at other schools. We used frequency standards for each type of activity: attending workshops with teachers from other schools at least 3 times since September; going to 3 or more committee meetings with teachers from other schools; and using electronic mail with teachers at other schools at least a half-dozen times. To be considered "high" on Beyond-School Contacts, two of those criteria needed to be met; a "medium" designation was given to teachers who met only one criterion. The vast majority of teachers attended workshops or conferences at some point during the year, and nearly one-half of those that did, attended at least three of them during the roughly six to eight months that transpired between the start of the school year and the point at which they answered their questionnaire. Fewer teachers participated on district or other-level committees, and fewer still used electronic mail to communicate with teachers from "other places." Of the teachers in the probability sample, 42% met the workshop attendance criterion, 28% met the committee meeting criterion, and 16% met the electronic mail criterion.

A majority of the teachers (53%) met at least one beyond-school contact criterion and 26% met two or three. Teachers who were rated "high" on the Within-School Interaction index were roughly twice as likely as teachers who met neither "high" nor "medium" standards for Within-School Interaction to meet each of the three Beyond-School Contact criteria.

Leadership

The third survey question asked about the teacher's involvement over the past three years in six types of leadership activities within the profession, including mentoring other teachers (2 measures), giving workshop presentations (2 measures), teaching college-level courses, and publishing. Overall, 19% of all teachers engaged in at least three of these six activities—qualifying them to be considered as possible "Teacher Leaders." Another 18% met the "medium" standard in this area (2 of the 6 activities).

One might argue that the leadership activities discussed in this one survey question provides a sufficiently comprehensive portrait of teacher peer leadership. However, teachers who only gave workshops, taught classes, and published articles, and who did not engage in frequent interaction with teacher peers at their own school or elsewhere, provide a rather limited, and abstract, form of leadership. Our measure of Teacher Leaders required activity in response to all three survey questions. It turned out that only 11% of those who met the "high" criterion for leadership (3 or more of the 6 types of leadership activities during the past three years) qualified as Teacher Leaders; the rest were either not sufficiently involved in two of the Beyond-School Contacts (conference attendance, committee work, or electronic mail communication with teachers in other places) or not sufficiently involved in informal substantive discussions and classroom observations at their own school. However, another 28% of those who were "high" in Leadership qualified for the second level of Professional Engagement (Teacher Professionals), by meeting the "medium" standard in each of the other two areas. Thus, overall, about 40% of the teachers who participated in several types of leadership activities also were engaged in both Within-School Interactions and had Beyond-School Contacts sufficient for them to be classified as "Professionally Engaged Teachers' teachers who met either the standards for a "Teacher Professional" or the more rigorous standards for a "Teacher Leader."

The differences in peer interaction and leadership behavior between the top two categories of Professional Engagement, Teacher Leaders and the Teacher Professionals, are not as great as the differences between both of those groups and the remaining teachers. In both groups, these are teachers who demonstrate a sense of their responsibility to engage in a regular interchange with an educational community beyond their classroom students. There is a difference in the forms and frequencies of their activities but the overall evidence points to a professional stance. Together, we refer to both categories of teachers as Professionally Engaged Teachers. There were also important differences among the teachers who did not meet "medium" standards on all three Professional Engagement measures and we indicated this by dividing this group into two as well. Teachers who were at the mean or higher on a combined index of all three survey questions, we termed Interactive Teachers. Teachers with scores below the mean, we termed Private Practice Teachers. All Interactive Teachers, as it turned out, scored medium or higher in at least one of the three areas and nearly 80% of them scored "high" in at least one area. However, in at least one area, Interactive Teachers failed to meet a medium standard. Thus, their teaching practice may involve professional dialog with teachers at their school, or collaboration beyond their school, or leadership activities, but not all three. On the other hand, almost half of all Private Practice Teachers did not meet even medium standards in any area and 85% of them did not meet a "high" standard in any area.

In summary, then, using a set of three survey questions and their 15 different empirical indicators, we divided teachers into four categories representing increasing levels of Professional Engagement. Overall, only 2% of teachers in our nationally representative (probability) sample met the criteria for being a Teacher Leader. Another 10% fell into the Teacher Professional Category. In contrast, more than half (58%) (partly by definition, but confirmed by the nature of their reports of their teaching practice) were classed as Private Practice Teachers. The remaining 29% of probability sample teachers fall into the intermediate category, which we term Interactive Teachers. Such teachers do engage in substantive interaction with other teachers, but do not do so both in school and beyond school and in a way that their professional leadership is publicly visible.

Given that nearly one-half of the teachers in the Teaching, Learning, and Computing survey sample were drawn from outside of the probability sample (i.e., 45% were from schools participating in instructional reform programs or in schools with a substantial density of computer technologies), it is not surprising that Professionally Engaged Teachers constitute a somewhat larger percentage of teachers in the full sample than in the probability sample alone (15% vs. 12%). Although so far this paper has focused on the probability sample of teachers, most of the remaining data draws from both the probability and purposive samples in our database—thus disproportionately including teachers from schools involved in instructional reform programs and from schools with a high level of computer technology. The reason for combining both samples of teachers into a single analysis was to enable us to divide the sample into small segments (e.g., by subject taught) and still be able to identify differences between higher and lower levels of Professional Engagement. Where patterns appeared to sharply differ between the probability and purposive samples, we retreated to the data on the probability sample alone.

The remainder of this report examines differences and similarities among the four types of teachers defined by their level of Professional Engagement. Primarily, we are looking "backwards," at differences in teachers' own backgrounds, teaching responsibilities, and teaching philosophies that might account for their different role orientations. We also look "sideways" to see whether Teacher Leaders teach differently than other teachers and whether they use computers differently in their teaching. And we examine students' differential access to Professionally Engaged Teachers by relating student socio-economic and achievement variables to the professional engagement of the teachers who teach them.

Personal Characteristics and Teaching Experience

Teacher Leaders, on the average, are about 5 years older and have had 5 years more teaching experience than the other teachers in the sample. While it makes sense that veteran teachers should be providing leadership, this finding runs contrary to assertions often made about teachers, such as that older teachers, educated at a time when teaching was seen as a more solitary activity, might be less likely to be involved in professional activities. Clearly, that is not always the case. In the overall sample, 66% of the respondents were female. However the most professionally engaged teachers—Teacher Leaders and Teacher Professionals—were even more likely to be female (74%).

Although relatively few teachers themselves graduated from "selective" colleges and universities (i.e., those whose entering freshman scored above 1100 on SATs), Teacher Leaders were more likely to do so than other groups of teachers (13% vs. 8%). In addition, the most professionally engaged teachers maintained higher grade point averages in college and were more likely to have graduate degrees than the rest of the teachers in the sample. When we combine four educational background variables into an index of "Educational Investment," we find that teachers with greater professional engagement have substantially higher average educational investment themselves. For example, the average Teacher Leader's Educational Investment score (0.49) would place him or her in the 69th percentile nationally. Teacher Professionals are also more educated than typical teachers in the sample (averaging in the 60th percentile). Private Practice Teachers are, in contrast, less well educated (45th percentile). Although there are likely to be many very good teachers who are isolated in their classrooms, this data suggests that those who close the door are teachers with less academic preparation than those who are engaged in professional activities.

Teaching Responsibilities

Teacher Leaders and Teacher Professionals were distributed proportionally across subject areas and grade levels in the national probability sample with one exception: Proportionately more computer education teachers met the criteria for these two highest levels of Professional Engagement. Thus, it appears that teachers who teach computer classes, as a whole, are more engaged in a collaborative culture than teachers from other subject areas. The Teacher Leaders and Professionals who were identified from the purposive sample—the reform program schools and schools with very high levels of technology—showed more variation by subject area. These schools appear to have proportionally more Professionally Engaged Teachers in other applied secondary subjects besides computer education (e.g., business and vocational education), and also in elementary self-contained classrooms.

Philosophy of Teaching

As a group, Professionally Engaged Teachers seem philosophically different from Private Practice Teachers. Teachers' responses to individual TLC survey questions suggest that Teacher Leaders and Teacher Professionals are more likely than other teachers to see good teaching in terms of facilitating student inquiry rather than directly transmitting knowledge. They are more likely to emphasize student engagement in learning and the "meaningfulness" of content than to be concerned about disseminating a specific externally mandated curriculum to unmotivated students. In fact, across a large number of survey questions about teaching philosophy, there was such a coherence in the differences in beliefs about good teaching between Professionally Engaged and Private Practice Teachers that one can truly say these groups espouse quite different teaching philosophies.

Educational Philosophy Index

Our measure of teaching philosophy comes from three survey questions, incorporating 13 individual prompts. In one question, teachers were asked to compare the likely effects on student learning of two teachers' contrasting approaches to classroom discussion. One approach represented traditional teacher-directed questioning based on prior reading; the other represented teacher-led discussion that provoked questions from the students themselves which the teacher then reflected back to them for further research. A second set of four questions presented paired comparisons of contrasting teaching philosophies. Each item presented a hypothetical personal statement of beliefs around issues such as curriculum coverage versus "meaning-making" and alternative classroom activity patterns (teacher-directed versus varying group activities). The third question involved a set of seven agree vs. disagree statements (6-point scales) including explaining the need for direct instruction in terms of the importance of providing students with background knowledge; arguing for the value of building instruction around problems with "clear, correct answers and—ideas that most students can grasp quickly"; and valuing student freedom of movement in the classroom for facilitating student initiative to learn.

An index was created by taking the mean of these 13 prompts, after equalizing item standard deviations (effectively creating standard scores for items). The alpha reliability for this index was .83, suggesting that a strong single dimension underlies these specific beliefs about good teaching. We term that dimension a "teaching philosophy," with a contrast between a "transmission" view of good teaching (direct instruction and repetitive skills practice around a fixed curriculum) and a "constructivist" view (knowledge construction through collaborative projects, and problem solving tasks.). A median score on this index suggests a teacher who is moderately constructivist in philosophy. For this report, the index was divided roughly into quartiles, with teachers in the lowest quartile classified as "most transmission-oriented" and those in the highest quartile as "most constructivist."

Teaching Philosophy and Professional Engagement

Only 3% of the Teacher Leaders fall in the most transmission-oriented quartile compared to 32% of the Private Practice Teachers, while 58% of the Teacher Leaders define their overall beliefs about good teaching in ways that suggest a strongly constructivist philosophy (compared to only 20% of Private Practice Teachers).

Student Clientele

Are Teacher Leaders more often found in "privileged" environments, at schools where students come from advantaged homes? And are they assigned to classes that disproportionately enroll students who are already more successful academically? In other words, if Teacher Leaders face different environmental conditions in their teaching, perhaps it is those factors that might account for their more constructivist orientation? On the contrary, however, we found little evidence that Teacher Leaders or Teacher Professionals are faced with different types of students than other teachers are.

The TLC data combined several different measures of school-level socio-economic advantage into a general index of socio-economic status (SES). Using this index, the correlation between teacher Professional Engagement and socio-economic status was .01. Combining the probability and purposive samples, 16% of the teachers from low-SES schools—the bottom quartile—were either Teacher Leaders or Teacher Professionals whereas in the other three quartiles, the percentages ranged between 14% and 15%.

In addition to a measure of socio-economic advantage, the TLC survey had one measure of the academic ability levels of students taught by each teacher. Teachers reported prior achievement levels of students in each class they taught. (Each class could be indicated as having at least a handful of students at as many as 5 different achievement levels; e.g., one class could be coded as "below-average," "average," and "very high" if a teacher believed students were at all such levels of prior achievement.) The estimates for each class were averaged across all classes a teacher taught.

On this dimension of the teaching context, Teacher Leaders did report some differences from the other three groups of teachers. In the purposive sample, Teacher Leaders were more likely to have classes of relatively high-ability students (35% did compared to 25% for the purposive sample as a whole). However, in the probability sample, the pattern was the opposite—Teacher Leaders were more likely to have students they rated as generally low achievers (20% did, versus 14% overall). For the full TLC sample, Professionally Engaged teachers did report somewhat higher average student achievement levels than other teachers, but the differences amounted to less than 10% of a standard deviation—much smaller than the differences we have been identifying for other variables. Thus, the general pattern is that teachers of different levels of Professional Engagement serve essentially similar students in terms of both socio-economic status and student achievement. Therefore, other findings, such as the relationship between Professional Engagement and a constructivist teaching philosophy, are not likely due to the kinds of students and schools encountered by Teacher Leaders compared to the experience of other teachers.

Teaching Practice

While "teaching philosophy" expresses teachers' beliefs about good teaching, what teachers do in actual classroom settings may be quite different. In the TLC study, we asked teachers about the frequency that they engaged in more than two dozen teaching practices. In this section we address the question of whether Professionally Engaged Teachers and Private Practice Teachers employ characteristically different practices in their teaching, even among those who teach the same subjects. We present selected results about individual teaching practices, and then discuss how these individual practices are combined into indices representing general approaches to teaching.

The survey items come from five survey questions which asked teachers to report about their instructional practices in one particular class that best represented their teaching. Each comparison is limited to teachers of one particular subject, one where the practice is fairly common. That helps in visualizing the nature of a teacher's instructional goals and what he or she might mean by using a specific teaching practice.

Professionally Engaged English teachers were more than twice as likely as Private Practice English teachers to have students work in teams to complete assignments (78% vs. 36%). They were also much more likely to have students write in a journal on at least a weekly basis (67% vs. 45%), and they were somewhat less likely to introduce a new unit by having students do introductory drills on background facts or skills. Among social studies teachers, Professionally Engaged Teachers were much more likely than Private Practice Teachers to have students work on long projects (72% vs. 33%) and to do meta-cognitive assessments of their own work (61% vs. 23%), while they were much less likely to lead their class in frequent whole-class recitation activities (27% vs. 61%) or to ask their students questions for the purpose of seeing if their students knew the correct answer (22% vs. 61%).

Professionally engaged science teachers were almost twice as likely as Private Practice science teachers to ask students questions in order to get students to relate their school work to their own personal experiences (74% vs. 40%) and they were more than twice as likely to have students work in small groups on a weekly basis to collectively solve a problem (66% vs. 28%). Secondary math teachers falling into the Professionally Engaged group were more likely than Private Practice math teachers to report that they had students work on problems with no obvious solution (54% vs. 35%), but clearly less likely to report that they asked students questions in order to see if they had done their homework (29% vs. 47%). Professionally Engaged elementary teachers (grades 4-6) were substantially more likely to have students decide on procedures for solving problems and more likely to introduce their current unit by having students discuss the topic in small groups.

Differences were also found for teachers of non-academic subjects. For example, among teachers of computer classes, many more Professionally Engaged Teachers than Private Practice Teachers said that at least monthly they had students make a product to be used by someone else (43% vs. 26%). Finally, among vocational education and fine arts teachers, those who met the criteria to be designated as Professionally Engaged were more than three times as likely to have students demonstrate their work to an outside audience as were Private Practice Teachers of the same subjects (56% to 18%). Again, we should point out that these differences were not necessarily the strongest ones in the data. Data were purposely examined only for one subject-matter area for each survey item—albeit an area where differences, if they existed, were likely to be most visible. Some of these differences apply across-the-board.That row shows that across teachers of all subjects, those who were the most Professionally Engaged were half-again as likely to say that their students did hands-on or laboratory activities on at least a weekly basis as did Private Practice Teachers (64% vs. 44%).

Pedagogy Index

How should we understand these differences? Based on our extensive exploratory factor analyses, it is clear that almost all of the teaching practices we examined fall along a continuum from a "direct instruction" approach to teaching to an approach based on an underlying knowledge-construction conception of teaching. Moreover, this dimension of teaching practice is highly correlated with the traditional versus constructivism dimension of teaching philosophy. Based on the factor analysis results, an index of Constructivist Pedagogy was constructed for each teacher based on their scores on 27 item prompts from five survey questions. Practices whose frequent use reflected instead a direct instruction approach were scored in reverse direction. The alpha reliability for this index was .86. The index was standardized separately for each subject-matter group of teachers, so as not to allow differential subject-matter relevance of the survey items to affect teachers' scores. In addition to using the specific scores on this Constructivist Pedagogy Index, the index was divided roughly into quartiles, with teachers in the lowest quartile classified as "direct instruction-oriented" based on the way they described what they did on a regular basis in a specific, current classroom context.

Professional Engagement and Constructivist Teaching Practice

As suggested by our results on individual survey items, when we combine all 27 practices into an index contrasting transmission-oriented practices with knowledge-construction ones, Professionally Engaged teachers turn out to be much more constructivist in practice than are Private Practice Teachers. Just as with teaching philosophy, a clear majority (57%) of the Teacher Leaders fall in the quartile that most reflects a knowledge construction approach to teaching while only 2% of the Teacher Leaders are located in the direct instruction quartile. In contrast, among Private Practice Teachers, twice as many fall into the most direct-instruction-oriented quartile as fall into the most knowledge-construction-oriented quartile.

The relationship between Professional Engagement and constructivist teaching practice is quite strong across teachers of every subject-matter category analyzed in the TLC survey.

For all seven subject-matter categories, the scores for Professionally Engaged Teachers were more than two-thirds of a standard deviation higher, suggesting that they are far more constructivist in their teaching than are Private Practice Teachers of the same subject. The largest differences are in the field of Social Studies, where Professionally Engaged Teachers scored an average of 1.35 standard deviations higher in the direction of constructivist practice than do Private Practice Teachers.

Components of Constructivist Pedagogy

Exploratory factor analysis suggested four empirically derived sub-components, which upon further reflection appear to represent two major overriding dimensions—(A) an emphasis on cognitively challenging tasks as opposed to routine low-level exercises; and (B) an emphasis on active engagement in learning versus a more limited and passive role for students. The "active learning" dimension of constructivist practice sub-divid`es into three empirically identifiable elements: (1) the use of student projects; (2) small group work; and (3) an infrequent use of direct instruction activities. The "cognitive challenge" aspect also can be classified into several elements (reflective writing activities, teacher questions calling for deep thinking, problem-solving tasks, and organization of classroom time to promote meaning-making among students) but these are more highly correlated with one another than with the elements of "active learning" and so are best analyzed as a single component.

Teacher Leaders demonstrate the most constructivist teaching practices; Teacher professionals, the next most; and Private Practice Teachers, the least. Although we found that more Professionally engaged teachers assign all types of constructivist activities more often than other teachers do, this was especially true of the use of student projects. Teacher Leaders scored nearly one full standard deviation above the mean score for all teachers in the TLC sample in their use of student projects.

Pedagogical Change

In addition to asking teachers about their current teaching practices, we also asked 50% of the teachers about the ways that their teaching practice had changed over the past three years. This retrospective self-assessment involved 16 separate items that asked about increased or decreased use of practices associated with constructivist teaching or with traditional teaching. Two subsets of eight items each were used with different teachers (i.e., one-fourth of the total sample answered one set; another one-fourth answered the other). The two short subsets of items (the 8 items asked to each group of teachers, each on a 4-point scale) produced indices with alpha reliability (.66 and .58) lower than the index of (current) Constructivist Pedagogy discussed above, but for our exploratory purposes they produced an adequate measure. The two 8-item indices asked to different subsets of respondents were combined and then categorized into four levels from "substantial constructivist change" to "little or no change or change towards a more traditional practice."

Changes in Pedagogy by Professional Engagement

Teacher Leaders and Teacher Professionals were much more likely to report having made substantial changes in their own pedagogy towards a more constructivist practice than were Private Practice Teachers. For example, 41% of the Teacher Leaders appear to have made substantial changes in many of the areas we asked about (or some change in most areas). In contrast, only 11% of the Private Practice Teachers reported that level of change during the past three years. Thus, not only are Professionally Engaged Teachers more constructivist in philosophy and in current practice than are teachers involved in little or no professional activity, but they are also more likely to report substantial movement towards a more constructivist practice during the past three years.

Computer Use

We turn now to a discussion of teachers' use of computers. Our central questions are whether teachers who are professionally engaged use computers more frequently than other teachers, and whether they use computers in ways that reflect their more constructivist orientation. Our principal focus is on instructional use by students during class time—how frequently teachers ask students to use computers, what types of software they have students use, and their educational objectives for student computer use. In addition, we employ a more comprehensive measure of teacher involvement with computers, one that incorporates teacher professional uses and their own technical expertise as well as their use of computers in instructional activities with students.

Relationship Between Professional Engagement and Computer Use

In nearly every subject-area of instruction, Teacher Leaders and Teacher Professionals are more likely to have their students use computers on a regular basis during class time than are Private Practice Teachers. For most subjects, they are also more likely than "Interactive Teachers" (the intermediate category of Professional Engagement) to give students regular (i.e., weekly) computer activities. The differences for the other academic subjects are smaller, but Professionally Engaged English and science teachers are twice as likely as Private Practice Teachers of the same subjects to assign computer work on a frequent basis.

Professionally Engaged Teachers use every type of software more than Private Practice Teachers. Even when only teachers who use computers for instruction are considered, the greater the teacher's professional engagement, the more frequently do students use a given type of software.

The greatest differences between Professionally Engaged Teachers and Private Practice teachers are in the former group's use of electronic mail, multimedia authoring software, and presentation software. Professionally Engaged Teachers use that software to enable students to communicate with other people and to produce products for an audience—activities closely associated with constructivist pedagogy. Not surprisingly, then, when teachers who used computers for instructional purposes were asked about their three most important objectives for using computers, Professionally Engaged Teachers selected more constructivist objectives than did the other groups of teachers. They were more likely than the other teachers who use computers in their classroom to have students use them to communicate with other people, analyze data, and learn to work collaboratively. They were less likely to use computers with the goal of having students learn computer skills, master basic academic skills, or learn to work by themselves. The differences are not as great as in our findings about software. Nevertheless, the Teacher Leaders, in particular, are twice as likely as Private Practice Teachers to have students use computers in order to communicate electronically and only half as likely to have them use computers for skills mastery purposes.

Exemplary Computer Users

The preceding evidence makes it clear that Professionally Engaged Teachers use a wider variety and more complex software with students than Private Practice Teachers do. They report objectives for student use of computers that go beyond learning using technology to teach technical skills or to simply reinforce memory. Those findings suggest that Professionally Engaged Teachers are more expert in using computers to facilitate complex academic work by students and may be more accomplished at integrating computer technology into their own professional lives. To examine in a more comprehensive way the extent that Professionally Engaged Teachers might differ from other teachers in their involvement with computers, we used factor analysis to identify a group of teachers we call "Exemplary Computer Users." We input into the factor analysis the data on the:

— Frequency of instructional use of each of 10 categories of software.

— Frequency and variety of teachers' professional use of computers.

— Degree of technical expertise they report in using computers and different computer platforms.

— Type and degree of access to computers and related technologies at work and home.

— Whether students used computers for each of several types of complex, integrative projects.

— Extent to which computer use has increased over the past five years, in several different ways.

Factor analysis of all these different indicators of teachers' involvement with computers produced three factors, which we labeled "Con structivist Instructional Use," "Frequent Simple Uses," and "Professional Use and Expertise." The factor Constructivist Instructional Use, for example, was most influenced by how frequently a teacher had students use email, presentation software, web browsers, multimedia authoring software, and complex projects using computers. The Frequent Simple Use score was most influenced by a teacher's use with students of word processing, skill games, and frequent use of computers in general. A high score on Professional Use and Expertise indicates a high number of self-reported computer skills, a sense of expertise on both Mac and Windows platforms, and the use of a wide variety of professional computer applications (e.g., accessing lesson materials from the Internet, using digital cameras for lesson preparation, corresponding with parents, and posting student work on the Web). Teachers scores on these three dimensions were combined, and, using a judgmental process, cutoff points were chosen that, in combination, selected 10% of all teachers as Exemplary Computer Users. Similar percentages (9% to 12%) at each school level and in subject-areas (other than computer and business education) were identified as exemplary.

Yet when we disaggregate teachers according to their level of Professional Engagement, rather remarkable differences appear. In particular, Teacher Leaders were 10 times as likely as Private Practice Teachers to be designated as Exemplary Computer Users. Forty percent of Teacher Leaders were also Exemplary Users, compared to only 4% of Private Practice Teachers. About one-fourth of Teacher Professionals were classed as Exemplary, six times as many as among Private Practice Teachers. Of the three component factors of this measure, Teacher Leaders are most different from other teachers in having students use constructivist-oriented tool software (mean z-score of +.88), and least different from other teachers in terms of frequent use of simple software (still more than one-half standard deviation higher than average, z=+.52). On Professional Use and Expertise, their superiority was extremely high (z=+.67), but not as high as on Constructivist Instructional Use.

Of all of the ways in which Professionally Engaged and Private Practice teachers might differ—in their backgrounds, teaching responsibilities, teaching philosophies, and teaching practices—none of them produced differences on the order of magnitude of this measure of Exemplary Computer Use. This suggests that there is a very strong connection between teacher leadership and sophisticated use of computers, in both teaching and professional life.

Teacher Leaders are much more likely than the typical teacher to have incorporated a wide variety of computer applications into their instructional practice and they are much more likely to have become competent users of computers themselves.

The magnitude of this association suggests that several different causal forces are operating—that teachers who act in professional ways are more motivated to master new technologies and more easily see the utility of computers in their work; that accomplishment in using technology in student lessons and in class preparation motivates teachers into sharing with peers their new skills; and, in a complementary way, that teachers seeking to learn to exploit computers in their work also seek out professional contacts as a means of attaining those skills. The huge association between computer expertise and professional leadership among teachers also helps to explain why the excitement about using computers one sees at professional meetings of teachers does not translate into widespread improvement across-the-board in teachers' use of technology: the participants at such conferences are professionals who are exploiting computers in their work, but they are an unrepresentative subset of purveyors of their craft. The real challenge for such leaders is to transfer their excitement and expertise to their peers who lack the same interest for involving themselves either in professional activities or in learning to master the application of computer resources to their instructional and work tasks.

Bibliography

Batya Friedman and Terry Winograd, eds., *Computing and Social Responsibility: A Collection of Course Syllabi, Computer Professionals for Social Responsibility*, 1990.

Donald Gotterbarn, "A 'Capstone' Course in Computer Ethics" in Terrell Ward Bynum, Walter Maner and John L. Fodor, eds., *Teaching Computer Ethics*, Research Center on Computing & Society, 1992.

Donn Parker, Susan Swope and Bruce N. Baker, Ethical Conflicts in Information and Computer Science, *Technology and Business*, QED Information Sciences, 1990.

Henwood, Flis, "Establishing gender perspectives on information technology: problems issues and opportunities", in E. Green, J. Owen and D. Pain (eds.), *Gendered by Design*, London: Taylor and Francis, 1993.

Hess, R., & I. Miura, "Gender differences in enrolment in computer camps and classes", *Sex Roles*, 13(3/4), 193-203, 1985.

Jane Robinett and Ramon Barquin, eds., *Computers and Ethics: A Sourcebook for Discussions*, Polytechnic Press, 1989.

Keith Miller, "Integrating Computer Ethics into the Computer Science Curriculum," *Computer Science Education*, Vol. 1, 1988, 37 - 52.

Jonsson, Ingrid, "Women in Education from a Swedish Perspective", in Julia Wright (ed.), *Education and Gender Equality*, London: The Falmer Press, 1992.

Klawe, M., and N. Levenson, "Women in computing: where are we now?", *Communications of the ACM,* January 1995, 38(1), 29-35, 1995.

Kling, R., and W. Sacchi, "The web of computing: computing technology as social organisation", *Advances in Computers,* 21, 3-85, 1982

Lightbody, P., G. Siann, R. Stocks and D. Walsh, "Motivation and attribution at secondary school: the role of gender", *Educational Studies,* 22(1), 13-25, 1996.

Tidjens, Kea G., "Gender segregation in IT occupations", *In Women Work and Computerisation: Proceedings of the 6th International IFIP Conference,* Bonn, Germany, May 24-27, 1997. A.F. Grundy, D. Kohler, V.Oechtering, U.Petersen (Eds), Germany: Springer, 1997.

Van Vonderen, M., and L. Dijkstra, "Women study technology: goals and restrictions", *International Journal of Science Education,* 9(3), pp 343-349, 1987.

Index

Advanced Research Projects Agency (ARPA) 124, 131

Assembly Language 88
Authentic communication 175

Classroom assignments 2
Classroom learning, 217
Computer conferencing 174
Computer program 79
Computer skills 2
Constructivist Instructional Use 270
Content area curriculum 1
Conventional higher education 179

Data Collection 4
Department of Defence (DOD) 124
Digital Equipment Corporation (DEC) 130
Distance learning 219
Distance education programs 225

Educational achievement 218
Educational association 1
Educational community 247

Fairly simple program 83
File Management 114
Fortran translator 100
Functional decomposition 9

Heterogeneity 226
High Level' Languages 94

Interface Message Processors (IMPs) 125
Information retrieval 31
Information technology literacy 3
Information technology skills 2
Initial classification 175
Instruction Register (IR) 76
Instructional delivery system 225
Instructional format 221
Integrated information skills programs 2
Integrated learning system 1

Job Control Language (JCL) 120

Memory management schemes 118
Mnemonic instruction names 84
Multifaceted components 174

Online learning 176
Online learning communities 173
Online telecommunications 223
Operating System (OS), 105
Organizational learning 219

Post-secondary education 1
Private Practice Teachers 249
Professional Engagement 259
Professional Practice 246

Quantitative synthesis 217
Quasi-experimental design 228

Retrospective self-assessment 266

Socio-Economic Status (SES) 260
Syntax rules 85
Systematic information process 2

Teacher-directed questioning 258
Technology literacy competencies 3
Technology-supported collaborative learning 220
Text-based transcripts 174
Time-consuming process 219
Transmission-oriented practices 264

World Wide Web (WWW) 223